George Gordon Byron

The Prisoner of Chillon

With selections from Childe Harold and Mazeppa

George Gordon Byron

The Prisoner of Chillon
With selections from Childe Harold and Mazeppa

ISBN/EAN: 9783744755054

Printed in Europe, USA, Canada, Australia, Japan

Cover: Foto ©ninafisch / pixelio.de

More available books at **www.hansebooks.com**

THE PRISONER OF CHILLON

WITH SELECTIONS FROM

CHILDE HAROLD AND MAZEPPA

BY

LORD BYRON

WITH INTRODUCTORY AND EXPLANATORY NOTES

NEW YORK AND NEW ORLEANS
UNIVERSITY PUBLISHING COMPANY
1896

COPYRIGHT, 1896, BY
UNIVERSITY PUBLISHING COMPANY

** 1752

Press of J. J. Little & Co.
Astor Place, New York

INTRODUCTION.

George Gordon Noel Byron was born in London on January 22, 1788. His father was John Byron, a captain in the British army, and nephew of Lord William Byron of Newstead Abbey, Nottingham, England. His mother was Catherine Gordon, daughter of George Gordon, a gentleman of high family and considerable landed estate in Aberdeenshire, Scotland. Captain Byron was a man of disreputable character and extravagant habits. He squandered nearly all his wife's means, and when he died in 1792 there was but a small income left to support the widow and her infant child, then living in the city of Aberdeen.

Lord William Byron died in 1798. As he had no children, his property and title descended to his grandnephew, George, who thus at the age of ten years became Lord Byron. The mother and son then removed to Newstead, the ancient home of the Byrons, and soon afterwards the young lord was sent to the famous school of Harrow, and subsequently to Trinity College, Cambridge. To his mother's injudicious indulgence has been partly attributed the waywardness that marked his subsequent career.

Lord Byron was not what would be called a good student. At Harrow, as he tells us himself, he was "always cricketing, rebelling, fighting, and in all manner of mischiefs." But though he neglected his class studies, he was a great reader of books, particularly books of history, biography, poetry, and fiction. Before he was fifteen years of age he had read histories of all the principal countries of the world, lives of most of the celebrated men of ancient and modern times, and nearly all the British poets. To this early and extensive study of English writers, as one of his biographers remarks, may be attributed that mastery over his own language with which Lord Byron came equipped into the field of literature, and which enabled him as fast as his youthful fancies sprung up to clothe them in words worthy of their beauty.

Byron began writing poetry at the age of twelve, and at the age of nineteen he published a collection of his verses under the title, "Hours of Idleness." These youthful productions, not of very high merit, were severely criticised by the "Edinburgh Review." Byron replied in the "English Bards and Scotch Reviewers," in which he fiercely attacked not only the editors of the "Review" but many of the best known literary men of the country. Soon after the publication of this poem he left England on a travelling tour, during which he visited Portugal and Spain, Greece, Turkey, and Asia Minor. One of the events of the tour was the famous swim across the Hellespont, from Sestos on the European to Abydos on the Asiatic side, a feat which Byron himself thus mentions in a letter to a friend in England:

"This morning [May 3, 1810] I swam from Sestos to Abydos. The immediate distance is not above a mile, but the current renders it hazardous. I attempted it a week ago, and failed, owing to the north wind and the wonderful rapidity of the tide, though I have been from my childhood a strong swimmer. But this morning being calmer, I succeeded, and crossed the 'broad Hellespont' in an hour and ten minutes."

Shortly after his return to England he published the first two cantos of "Childe Harold," which he had written while abroad. The work was received with universal applause, and Byron was at once recognized as a poet of the first rank. "I woke one morning," says he in his memoranda, "and found myself famous."

Within the next two years he wrote "The Giaour," "The Bride of Abydos," "The Corsair," and "Lara," brilliant poems, containing many vivid pictures of scenes of beauty with which the author had become familiar during his travels in the East. About this time (1815) the poet married Miss Milbanke, a lady of rank and fortune, daughter of Sir Ralph Milbanke. The union was brief and unhappy. One year after their marriage they separated, and Byron left England never to return.

The remainder of the poet's life was spent chiefly in Switzerland and Italy, amid those beauties of nature and art which he describes so well in his poems. His industry in literary work during these years (from 1816 to 1823) was remarkable. Besides completing "Childe Harold," he produced a great number of poems, translations, and plays, including "The Prisoner of Chillon," "Manfred," "Beppo," "Mazeppa," "The Lament of Tasso," "Sardanapalus," "The Vision of Judgment," "Heaven and Earth," "Cain," "Werner," "The Island," "Don Juan," and several others.

Byron was an ardent lover of liberty, and it was this passion which led him into the enterprise that cost him his life. In 1823 he sailed to Greece to join the patriots there who were at the time engaged in a struggle to free their country from the oppressive rule of Turkey, to which it had been subject since the fifteenth century, when the Turks, or Ottomans, a warlike people of Asia, led by their King, or Sultan, Mohammed II., besieged and captured Constantinople, conquered a great part of southeastern Europe, including the countries now known as Turkey and Greece. The Greeks made many attempts to shake off the yoke of Turkey. With the aid of Russia, France, and England they succeeded in 1828, and since 1832 their country has been an independent kingdom. The action of Lord Byron had much to do in arousing European and American sympathy in their behalf. He flung himself into the movement with the enthusiasm of a generous nature, giving a large sum of money, as well as his personal service, in aid of the cause of Greek independence. But he did not live to witness its success. A severe cold, contracted through exposure to rain, brought on an attack of fever and rheumatism, of which he died at Missolonghi, Greece, on April 19, 1824, speaking in his last moments of his wife and only child, a daughter whom he tenderly loved. His body was conveyed to England, and interred in the family vault in the church of Hucknall, near Newstead.

Byron was a man of hot and violent temper, which was aggravated by domestic troubles, as well as by physical infirmity, an accident at his birth having injured one of his feet and caused lameness for life. The effect on his mind and character of these and other unfavorable circumstances is manifest in much of his writing. Still more, however, are the noble qualities of the man shown forth in his works—his affectionate nature, his hatred of wrong, his love of right and justice, and his sympathy with the oppressed in every land.

The Prisoner of Chillon

Mazeppa .

Childe Harold . .

THE PRISONER OF CHILLON.

A FABLE.

SONNET ON CHILLON.

ETERNAL Spirit of the chainless Mind!
  Brightest in dungeons, Liberty! thou art.
  For there thy habitation is the heart—
The heart which love of thee alone can bind;
And when thy sons to fetters are consign'd—
  To fetters, and the damp vault's dayless gloom,
  Their country conquers with their martyrdom,
And Freedom's fame finds wings on every wind.
Chillon! thy prison is a holy place,
  And thy sad floor an altar—for 'twas trod,
Until his very steps have left a trace,
  Worn, as if thy cold pavement were a sod,
By Bonnivard!¹ May none those marks efface!
  For they appeal from tyranny to God.

Byron wrote this poem in 1816, at a small inn, in the village of Ouchy, near Lausanne, a city of Switzerland, on the shore of Lake Geneva (also called Lake Leman). The castle and fortress of Chillon, which was for a long time a state prison, is at the east end of the lake. It is situated on a rock which is almost entirely surrounded by deep water and connected with the shore by a wooden bridge. The prisoners introduced in the poem are fictitious persons, suggested to the imagination of the poet by the appearance of the isolated castle, and no doubt by his reading of the sufferings to which many people were subjected for their religious opinions in past times when the principle of liberty of conscience was little understood or respected.

I.

My hair is gray, but not with years,
  Nor grew it white
  In a single night,
As men's have grown from sudden fears:

---

¹ François de Bonnivard (born 1496) was the patriot defender of the Republic of Geneva (Switzerland) against the Duke of Savoy, who imprisoned him for six years in the Castle of Chillon, the last four in that subterranean vault which the genius of Byron has made famous.

My limbs are bow'd, though not with toil,
   But rusted with a vile repose,
For they have been a dungeon's spoil ;
   And mine has been the fate of those
To whom the goodly earth and air
Are bann'd, and barr'd—forbidden fare ;
But this was for my father's faith :
I suffer'd chains and courted death :
That father perish'd at the stake [1]
For tenets [2] he would not forsake ;
And for the same his lineal race
In darkness found a dwelling place.
We were seven—who now are one ;
   Six in youth, and one in age,
Finish'd as they had begun,
   Proud of Persecution's rage ;
One in fire, and two in field, [3]
Their belief with blood have seal'd ;
Dying as their father died,
For the God their foes denied :
Three were in a dungeon cast,
Of whom this wreck [4] is left the last.

II.

There are seven pillars of Gothic mold [5]
In Chillon's dungeons deep and old ;
There are seven columns, massy and gray,
Dim with a dull imprison'd ray,
A sunbeam which hath lost its way,
And through the crevice and the cleft
Of the thick wall is fallen and left,

---

[1] the piece of wood to which a person condemned to death by fire was bound while burning.
[2] religious opinions.
[3] the battle-field.
[4] the prisoner.
[5] in the Gothic style—with pointed arches.

Creeping o'er the floor so damp,
Like a marsh's meteor lamp:[1]
And in each pillar there is a ring,
 And in each ring there is a chain:
That iron is a cankering thing,
 For in these limbs its teeth remain,
With marks that will not wear away,
Till I have done with this new day,
Which now is painful to these eyes,
Which have not seen the sun so rise
For years—I cannot count them o'er,
I lost their long and heavy score,
When my last brother droop'd and died,
And I lay living by his side.

III.

They chain'd us each to a column stone,
And we were three—yet, each alone;
We could not move a single pace,
We could not see each other's face,
But with that pale and livid light
That made us strangers in our sight:
And thus together, yet apart—
Fetter'd in hand, but joined in heart—
'Twas still some solace, in the dearth
Of the pure elements of earth,
To hearken to each other's speech,
And each turn comforter to each,
With some new hope, or legend old,
Or song heroically bold;
But even these at length grew cold.
Our voices took a dreary tone,
An echo of the dungeon-stone,

---
[1] the phosphorus that shines from a marsh, popularly called "will-o'-the-wisp."

A grating sound—not full and free
As they of yore were wont to be:
It might be fancy—but to me
They never sounded like our own.

IV.

I was the eldest of the three,
And to uphold and cheer the rest
I ought to do—and did my best—
And each did well in his degree.
  The youngest, whom my father loved,
Because our mother's brow was given
To him,[1] with eyes as blue as heaven,
  For him my soul was sorely moved:
And truly might it be distrest
To see such bird in such a nest;
For he was beautiful as day—
  (When day was beautiful to me
  As to young eagles, being free)—
  A polar day, which will not see
A sunset till its summer's gone,[2]
  Its sleepless summer of long light,
The snow-clad offspring of the sun:
  And thus he was as pure and bright,
And in his natural spirit gay,
With tears for nought but others' ills,
And then they flow'd like mountain rills,
Unless he could assuage the woe
Which he abhorr'd to view below.

V.

The other was as pure of mind,
But form'd to combat with his kind;

---

[1] he resembled his mother in face.
[2] at the poles the sun never sets during the summer months.

Strong in his frame, and of a mood
Which 'gainst the world in war had stood,[1]
And perish'd in the foremost rank
  With joy :—but not in chains to pine;
His spirit wither'd with their clank.
  I saw it silently decline—
  And so perchance in sooth did mine;
But yet I forced it on to cheer
Those relics of a home so dear.
He was a hunter of the hills,
  Had follow'd there the deer and wolf:
To him this dungeon was a gulf,
And fetter'd feet the worst of ills.

VI.

Lake Leman lies by Chillon's walls :
A thousand feet in depth below
Its massy waters meet and flow;
Thus much the fathom-line was sent
From Chillon's snow-white battlement,
  Which round about the wave enthralls;
A double dungeon wall and wave
Have made—and like a living grave.
Below the surface of the lake
The dark vault lies wherein we lay,
We heard it ripple night and day;
Sounding o'er our heads it knock'd ;
And I have felt the winter's spray
Wash through the bars when winds were high
And wanton[2] in the happy sky.
  And then the very rock hath rock'd,
  And I have felt it shake, unshock'd,
Because I could have smiled to see
The death that would have set me free.

---

[1] would gladly have stood.   [2] blowing freely without constraint.

VII.

I said my nearer brother pined,
I said his mighty heart declined,
He loathed and put away his food;
It was not that 'twas coarse and rude,
For we were used to hunter's fare,
And for the like had little care;
The milk drawn from the mountain goat
Was changed for water from the moat.
Our bread was such as captives' tears
Have moisten'd many a thousand years,
Since man first pent his fellow-men
Like brutes within an iron den:
But what were these to us or him?
These wasted not his heart or limb;
My brother's soul was of that mold
Which in a palace had grown cold,
Had his free breathing been denied
The range of the steep mountain's side;
But why delay the truth?—he died.
I saw, and could not hold his head,
Nor reach his dying hand—nor dead,
Though hard I strove, but strove in vain,
To rend and gnash my bonds in twain.
He died—and they unlock'd his chain
And scoop'd for him a shallow grave
Even from the cold earth of our cave.
I begg'd them, as a boon, to lay
His corse in dust whereon the day
Might shine—it was a foolish thought,
But then within my brain it wrought,
That even in death his freeborn breast
In such a dungeon could not rest.
I might have spared my idle prayer—
They coldly laughed—and laid him there,

The flat and turfless earth above
The being we so much did love;
His empty chain above it leant
Such murder's fitting monument!

VIII.

But he, the favorite and the flower,
Most cherish'd since his natal hour,[1]
His mother's image in fair face,
The infant love of all his race,
His martyr'd father's dearest thought,
My latest care, for whom I sought
To hoard my life, that his might be
Less wretched now, and one day free;
He, too, who yet had held untired
A spirit natural or inspired—
He, too, was struck, and day by day,
Was wither'd on the stalk away.
Oh God! it is a fearful thing
To see the human soul take wing
In any shape, in any mood:
I've seen it rushing forth in blood,
I've seen it on the breaking ocean
Strive with a swoln convulsive motion,
I've seen the sick and ghastly bed
Of Sin delirious with its dread:
But these were horrors—this was woe
Unmix'd with such—but sure and slow:
He faded, and so calm and meek,
So softly worn, so sweetly weak,
So tearless, yet so tender—kind,
And grieved for those he left behind;
With all the while a cheek whose bloom
Was as a mockery of the tomb,

[1] hour of birth.

Whose tints as gently sunk away
As a departing rainbow's ray—
An eye of most transparent light,
That almost made the dungeon bright,
And not a word of murmur—not
A groan o'er his untimely lot,—
A little talk of better days,
A little hope my own to raise,
For I was sunk in silence—lost
In this last loss, of all the most;
And then the sighs he would suppress
Of fainting nature's feebleness.
More slowly drawn, grew less and less;
I listen'd, but I could not hear—
I call'd, for I was wild with fear;
I knew 'twas hopeless, but my dread
Would not be thus admonished;
I call'd, and thought I heard a sound—
I burst my chain with one strong bound,
And rush'd to him :—I found him not.
I only stirr'd in this black spot.
I only lived—*I* only drew
The accursed breath of dungeon dew;
The last—the sole—the dearest link
Between me and the eternal brink,
Which bound me to my failing race,
Was broken in this fatal place.¹
One on the earth, and one beneath—
My brothers—both had ceased to breathe.
I took that hand which lay so still,
Alas! my own was full as chill;
I had not strength to stir, or strive,
But felt that I was still alive—

---

¹ "The gentle decay and gradual extinction of the youngest life is the most tender and beautiful passage in the poem."—*Jeffrey.*

A frantic feeling, when we know
That what we love shall ne'er be so.
  I know not why
  I could not die,
I had no earthly hope but faith,
And that forbade a selfish death.

IX.

What next befell me then and there
  I know not well—I never knew.—
First came the loss of light and air,
  And then of darkness too:
I had no thought, no feeling—none—
Among the stones I stood a stone,
And was, scarce conscious what I wist,[1]
As shrubless crags within the mist;
For all was blank, and bleak, and gray,
It was not night—it was not day,
It was not even the dungeon-light,
So hateful to my heavy sight,
But vacancy absorbing space,
And fixedness—without a place:
There were no stars—no earth—no time—
No check—no change—no good—no crime—
But silence, and a stirless breath
Which neither was of life nor death;
A sea of stagnant idleness,
Blind, boundless, mute, and motionless!

X.

A light broke in upon my brain,—
  It was the carol of a bird;
It ceased, and then it came again,
  The sweetest song ear ever heard,

[1] knew.

And mine was thankful till my eyes
Ran over with the glad surprise.
And they that moment could not see
I was the mate of misery;
But then by dull degrees came back
My senses to their wonted track,
I saw the dungeon walls and floor
Close slowly round me as before,
I saw the glimmer of the sun
Creeping as it before had done,
But through the crevice where it came
That bird was perch'd, as fond and tame,
   And tamer than upon the tree;
A lovely bird, with azure wings,
And song that said a thousand things,
   And seem'd to say them all for me!
I never saw its like before,
I ne'er shall see its likeness more.
It seem'd, like me, to want a mate,
But was not half so desolate,
And it was come to love me when
None lived to love me so again,
And cheering from my dungeon's brink,
Had brought me back to feel and think.
I know not if it late were free,
   Or broke its cage to perch on mine,
But knowing well captivity,
   Sweet bird! I could not wish for thine!
Or if it were, in winged guise,
A visitant from Paradise;
For—Heaven forgive that thought! the while
Which made me both to weep and smile—
I sometimes deem'd that it might be
My brother's soul come down to me;
But then at last away it flew,

And then 'twas mortal—well I knew,
For he would never thus have flown,
And left me twice so doubly lone,—
Lone—as the corse within its shroud,
Lone—as a solitary cloud.
   A single cloud on a sunny day,
While all the rest of heaven is clear,
A frown upon the atmosphere,
That hath no business to appear
   When skies are blue, and earth is gay.

XI.

A kind of change came in my fate,
My keepers grew compassionate.
I know not what had made them so,
They were inured to sights of woe,
But so it was:—my broken chain
With links unfasten'd did remain,
And it was liberty to stride
Along my cell from side to side.
And up and down, and then athwart,
And tread it over every part;
And round the pillars one by one,
Returning where my walk begun,
Avoiding only, as I trod,
My brothers' graves without a sod;
For if I thought with heedless tread
My step profaned their lowly bed.
My breath came gaspingly and thick,
And my crush'd heart fell blind and sick.

XII.

I made a footing in the wall.
   It was not therefrom to escape,
For I had buried one and all,
   Who loved me in a human shape;

And the whole earth would henceforth be
A wider prison unto me:
No child—no sire—no kin had I,
No partner in my misery;
I thought of this, and I was glad
For thought of them had made me mad;
But I was curious to ascend
To my barr'd windows, and to bend
Once more, upon the mountains high,
The quiet of a loving eye.

XIII.

I saw them—and they were the same,
They were not changed like me in frame;
I saw their thousand years of snow
On high—their wide, long lake below,
And the blue Rhone [1] in fullest flow:
I heard the torrents leap and gush
O'er channell'd rock and broken bush;
I saw the white-wall'd distant town,
And whiter sails go skimming down;
And then there was a little isle,[2]
Which in my very face did smile,
　The only one in view.
A small green isle, it seem'd no more,
Scarce broader than my dungeon floor,
But in it there were three tall trees,
And o'er it blew the mountain breeze,
And by it there were waters flowing,
And on it there were young flowers growing,
　Of gentle breath and hue.
The fish swam by the castle wall,
And they seem'd joyous each and all:

---

[1] The river Rhone flows through Lake Geneva.

[2] There is a small island between the entrances of the Rhone and Villeneuve, a town at the extremity of the lake.

The eagle rode the rising blast,
Methought he never flew so fast,
As then to me he seem'd to fly,
And then new tears came in my eye,
And I felt troubled—and would fain
I had not left my recent chain.
And when I did descend again,
The darkness of my dim abode
Fell on me as a heavy load;
It was as is a new-dug grave,·
Closing o'er one we sought to save;
And yet my glance, too much oppress'd,
Had almost need of such a rest.

XIV.

It might be months, or years, or days,
　I kept no count—I took no note,
I had no hope my eyes to raise
　And clear them of their dreary mote;
At last men came to set me free,
　I ask'd not why, and reck'd not where;
It was at length the same to me,
Fetter'd or fetterless to be—
　I learn'd to love despair.
And thus when they appear'd at last,
And all my bonds aside were cast,
These heavy walls to me had grown
A hermitage—and all my own!
And half I felt as they were come
To tear me from a second home:
With spiders I had friendship made,
And watch'd them in their sullen trade;
Had seen the mice by moonlight play,
And why should I feel less than they?

We were all inmates of one place,
And I, the monarch of each race,
Had power to kill—yet, strange to tell!
In quiet we had learn'd to dwell:
My very chains and I grew friends,
So much a long communion tends
To make us what we are :—even I
Regain'd my freedom with a sigh.

MAZEPPA.

This poem is founded on historical facts. Mazeppa was a native of Poland. In his youth he became a page in the service of John Casimir, the king of that country. For an offence against a Polish count he was bound naked to the back of a wild horse, his head turned to its tail, and the animal was then sent off, leaving the unfortunate Mazeppa to his fate. He afterwards became a chief among the Cossacks, a semi-barbarous people of southern Russia. He joined Charles XII., the famous King of Sweden, in his war with Peter the Great, Czar of Russia, and was present at the battle of Pultowa (Russia) in 1709, in which Charles was defeated.

On these facts the genius and imagination of Byron have constructed the thrilling story represented in the poem as having been related by Mazeppa to King Charles, while resting in a forest on their retreat after the disastrous battle.

I.

'TWAS after dread Pultowa's day,
　　When fortune left the royal Swede,
Around a slaughter'd army lay,
　　No more to combat and to bleed.
The power and glory of the war,
　　Faithless as their vain votaries, men,
Had pass'd to the triumphant Czar,
　　And Moscow's [1] walls were safe again,
Until a day more dark and drear,
And a more memorable year,[2]
Should give to slaughter and to shame
A mightier host and haughtier name:[3]
A greater wreck, a deeper fall,
A shock to one—a thunderbolt to all.

[1] Moscow was formerly the capital of Russia.

[2] the year 1812, when Napoleon Bonaparte invaded Russia and entered Moscow with a great army. He soon found, however, that he had conquered nothing but a heap of ashes, the Russians having set fire to the city on the night of his arrival to force the invaders to retire. On their retreat from the country, thousands of the French perished of cold and hunger, Napoleon himself escaping only with much difficulty.

[3] Napoleon and his army.

II.

Such was the hazard of the die![1]
The wounded Charles was taught to fly
By day and night through field and flood,
Stain'd with his own and subjects' blood;
For thousands fell that flight to aid:
And not a voice was heard t' upbraid
Ambition in his humbled hour,
When truth had naught to dread from power.
His horse was slain, and Gieta[2] gave
His own—and died the Russians' slave.
This too sinks after many a league
Of well-sustain'd but vain fatigue;
And in the depths of forests, darkling
The watch-fires in the distance sparkling—
   The beacons of surrounding foes—
A king must lay his limbs at length.
   Are these the laurels and repose
For which the nations strain their strength?
They laid him by a savage tree,
In outworn nature's agony;
His wounds were stiff—his limbs were stark—
The heavy hour was chill and dark;
The fever in his blood forbade
A transient slumber's fitful aid:
And thus it was; but yet through all,
Kinglike the monarch bore his fall,
And made, in this extreme of ill,
His pangs the vassals[3] of his will:
All silent and subdued were they,
As once the nations round him lay.

---

[1] singular of dice, little cubes used in games of chance. War is here likened to a game played with dice.

[2] An officer of Charles XII.

[3] slaves.

III.

A band of chiefs!—alas! how few,
    Since but the fleeting of a day
Had thinn'd it; but this wreck was true
    And chivalrous:[1] upon the clay
Each sate him down, all sad and mute,
    Beside his monarch and his steed,
For danger levels man and brute,
    And all are fellows in their need.
Among the rest, Mazeppa made
His pillow in an old oak's shade—
Himself as rough, and scarce less old,
The Ukraine's Hetman [2] calm and bold;
But first, outspent with this long course,
The Cossack prince rubb'd down his horse,
And made for him a leafy bed.
    And smooth'd his fetlocks and his mane,
    And slack'd his girth, and stripp'd his rein,
And joy'd to see how well he fed;
For until now he had the dread
His wearied courser might refuse
To browse beneath the midnight dews:
But he was hardy as his lord,
And little cared for bed and board;
But spirited and docile too,
Whate'er was to be done, would do.
Shaggy and swift, and strong of limb,
All Tartar-like [3] he carried him;
Obey'd his voice, and came to call,
And knew him in the midst of all:

[1] brave and loyal.
[2] Mazeppa was hetman, or commander-in-chief, of the Cossacks of Ukraine, a district of southern Russia.
[3] Tartary was the name given at one time to the countries of central Asia and eastern Europe. The Tartars were famous as horsemen and hunters.

Though thousands were around,—and Night,
Without a star, pursued her flight,—
That steed from sunset until dawn
His chief would follow like a fawn.

IV.

This done, Mazeppa spread his cloak,
And laid his lance beneath his oak,
Felt if his arms in order good
The long day's march had well withstood—
If still the powder fill'd the pan,
And flints unloosen'd kept their lock [1]—
His sabre's hilt and scabbard felt,
And whether they had chafed his belt—
And next the venerable man,
From out his haversack and can,[2]
Prepared and spread his slender stock [3]
And to the monarch and his men
The whole or portion offer'd then
With far less of inquietude
Than courtiers [4] at a banquet would.
And Charles of this his slender share
With smiles partook a moment there,
To force of cheer a greater show,
And seem above both wounds and woe;
And then he said—" Of all our band,
Though firm of heart and strong of hand,
In skirmish, march, or forage, none
Can less have said or more have done
Than thee, Mazeppa! On the earth
So fit a pair had never birth,

---

[1] Before the invention of the percussion cap, and cartridge, guns were fired by a spark struck by a flint and steel attached to the lock of the weapon, the powder being placed in a pan where it caught the spark.
[2] soldier's bag and drinking can.   [3] of eatables.
[4] persons who attend the courts of kings.

Since Alexander's[1] days till now,
As thy Bucephalus and thou:
All Scythia's[2] fame to thine should yield
For pricking on o'er flood and field."
Mazeppa answer'd—"Ill betide[3]
The school wherein I learn'd to ride!"
Quoth Charles—"Old Hetman, wherefore so,
Since thou hast learn'd the art so well?"
Mazeppa said—"'Twere long to tell;
And we have many a league to go,
With every now and then a blow,
And ten to one at least the foe,
Before our steeds may graze at ease,
Beyond the swift Borysthenes:[4]
And, sire,[5] your limbs have need of rest,
And I will be the sentinel
Of this your troop."—"But I request,"
Said Sweden's monarch, "thou wilt tell
This tale of thine, and I may reap,
Perchance, from this the boon of sleep;
For at this moment from my eyes
The hope of present slumber flies."

"Well, sire, with such a hope I'll track
My seventy years of memory back:
I think 'twas in my twentieth spring,—
Ay, 'twas,—when Casimir was king—
John Casimir,[6]—I was his page
Six summers in my earlier age;

---

[1] Alexander the Great, a king of Macedon (north of Greece), and a celebrated conqueror, born 356 B.C. He had a famous horse named Bucephalus.
[2] Scythia, anciently the name of southern Russia.
[3] may evil happen to.
[4] ancient name of the Dnieper (*pron.* nee-per), a river of Russia, flowing into the Black Sea.
[5] a word of honor used in addressing kings.
[6] see Introductory Note.

A learned monarch, faith! was he,
And most unlike your majesty:
He made no wars, and did not gain
New realms to lose them back again;
   .   .   .   .   .

He was the Polish Solomon,[1]
So sung his poets, all but one,
Who, being unpension'd, made a satire,
And boasted that he could not flatter.
It was a court of jousts[2] and mimes,[3]
Where every courtier tried at rhymes;
Even I for once produced some verses,
And sign'd my odes 'Despairing Thyrsis.'[4]
There was a certain Palatine,[5]
  A count of far and high descent,
Rich as a salt[6] or silver mine:
And he was proud, ye may divine,
  As if from heaven he had been sent:
He had such wealth in blood and ore
  As few could match beneath the throne;
And he would gaze upon his store,
And o'er his pedigree would pore,
Until by some confusion led,
Which almost look'd like want of head,
He thought their merits[7] were his own.
His wife was not of his opinion;
  His junior she by thirty years,
Grew daily tired of his dominion;
   .   .

---

[1] meaning that he was a wise prince like Solomon, King of Israel.
[2] mock battles.
[3] dramatic plays.
[4] name sometimes given by ancient poets to shepherds or herdsmen.
[5] count.
[6] the wealth of Poland consisted greatly of salt mines.
[7] the merits of his ancestors.

V.

"I was a goodly stripling then;
  At seventy years I so may say,
That there were few, or [1] boys or men,
  Who, in my dawning time of day,
Of vassal or of knight's degree,
Could vie in vanities with me;
For I had strength, youth, gaiety,
A port,[2] not like to this ye see,
But smooth, as all is rugged now;
  For time, and care, and war have plow'd
My very soul from out my brow;
  And thus I should be disavow'd
By all my kind and kin could they
Compare my day and yesterday;
This change was wrought, too, long ere age
Had ta'en my features for his page:
With years, ye know, have not declined
My strength, my courage, or my mind,
Or at this hour I should not be
Telling old tales beneath a tree,
With starless skies my canopy.
  But let me on. Theresa's form—
Methinks it glides before me now,
Between me and yon chestnut's bough,
  The memory is so quick and warm
And yet I find no words to tell
The shape of her I loved so well.
She had the Asiatic eye,
  Such as our Turkish neighborhood
  Hath mingled with our Polish blood,
Dark as above us is the sky;
But through it stole a tender light,
Like the first moonrise of midnight,

---

[1] either.   [2] appearance and manner.

Large, dark, and swimming in the stream,
Which seem'd to melt to its own beam;
All love, half languor, and half fire,
Like saints that at the stake expire,
And lift their raptured looks on high,
As though it were a joy to die.
A brow like a midsummer lake,
   Transparent with the sun therein,
When waves no murmur dare to make,
   And heaven beholds her face within.
A cheek and lip—but why proceed?
I loved her then—I love her still;
And such as I am, love indeed
   In fierce extremes—in good and ill.
But still we love even in our rage
And haunted to our very age
With the vain shadow of the past,
As is Mazeppa to the last.

   .   .   .   .   .

VIII.

   .   .   .   .   .

But one fair night, some lurking spies
Surprised and seized us both.
The Count was something more than wroth—
I was unarm'd; but if in steel,
All cap-a-pie [1] from head to heel,
What 'gainst their numbers could I do?
'Twas near his castle, far away
   From city or from succor near,
And almost on the break of day;
I did not think to see another,
   My moments seem'd reduced to few;
And with one prayer to Mary Mother,[2]
   And it may be, a saint or two.

---

[1] head to foot.   [2] the mother of Christ, to whom prayers are offered in some churches.

As I resign'd me to my fate,
They led me to the castle gate:

              IX.

"'Bring forth the horse!'—the horse was brought,
In truth, he was a noble steed,
A Tartar of the Ukraine breed,
Who look'd as though the speed of thought
Were in his limbs; but he was wild,
   Wild as the wild deer, and untaught,
With spur and bridle undefiled—
'Twas but a day he had been caught;
And snorting, with erected mane,
And struggling fiercely, but in vain,
In the full foam of wrath and dread
To me the desert-born was led:
They bound me on, that menial throng;
Upon his back with many a thong:
Then loosed him with a sudden lash—
Away!—away!—and on we dash:
Torrents less rapid and less rash.

              X.

"Away!—away!—My breath was gone—
I saw not where he hurried on:
'Twas scarcely yet the break of day,
And on he foam'd—away!—away!—
The last of human sounds which rose,
As I was darted from my foes,
Was the wild shout of savage laughter,
Which on the wind came roaring after
A moment from that rabble rout:
With sudden wrath I wrench'd my head,
   And snapp'd the cord which to the mane
   Had bound my neck in lieu of rein,
And, writhing half my form about,

Howl'd back my curse ; but 'midst the tread,
The thunder of my courser's speed,
Perchance they did not hear or heed.
It vexes me—for I would fain
Have paid their insult back again.
I paid it well in after days:
There is not of that castle-gate,
Its drawbridge¹ and portcullis² weight,
Stone, bar, moat, bridge, or barrier left;
Nor of its fields a blade of grass,
 Save what grows on a ridge of wall,
Where stood the hearth-stone of the hall;
And many a time ye there might pass,
Nor dream that e'er that fortress was.
I saw its turrets in a blaze,
Their crackling battlements all cleft,
 And the hot lead pour down like rain
From off the scorch'd and blackening roof,
Whose thickness was not vengeance proof.³
 They little thought that day of pain,
When launch'd, as on the lightning's flash,
They bade me to destruction dash,
 That one day I should come again,
With twice five thousand horse, to thank
 The Count for his uncourteous ride.
They play'd me then a bitter prank,
When, with the wild horse for my guide,
They bound me to his foaming flank;
At length I play'd them one as frank—
For time at last sets all things even—
 And if we do but watch the hour,
There never yet was human power

---

¹ a bridge at the entrance to a fortress, which may be drawn up and let down at pleasure.
² a gate hung over the entrance to a fortress, which may be let down to keep out an enemy.   ³ sufficient defence against vengeance.

Which could evade, if unforgiven,
The patient search and vigil¹ long
Of him who treasures up a wrong.

XI.

"Away, away, my steed and I,
   Upon the pinions of the wind,
   All human dwellings left behind;
We sped like meteors through the sky,
When with its crackling sound the night
Is checker'd with the northern light.
Town—village—none were on our track,
   But a wild plain of far extent,
And bounded by a forest black;
   And, save the scarce-seen battlement
On distant heights of some strong hold,
Against the Tartars built of old,
No trace of man. The year before
A Turkish army had marched o'er;
And where the Spahi's² hoof hath trod,
The verdure flies the bloody sod:
The sky was dull, and dim, and gray,
   And a low breeze crept moaning by—
   I could have answer'd with a sigh—
But fast we fled, away, away,
And I could neither sigh nor pray;
And my cold sweat-drops fell like rain
Upon the courser's bristling mane;
But, snorting still with rage and fear,
He flew upon his far career:
At times I almost thought, indeed,
He must have slacken'd in his speed;
But no—my bound and slender frame
   Was nothing to his angry might,
And merely like a spur became;

¹ watch.   ² Spahis, Turkish cavalry.

Each motion which I made to free
My swoln limbs from their agony
  Increas'd his fury and affright:
I tried my voice,—'twas faint and low,
But yet he swerv'd as from a blow;
And, starting to each accent, sprang
As from a sudden trumpet's clang;
Meantime my cords were wet with gore,
Which, oozing through my limbs, ran o'er;
And in my tongue the thirst became
A something fiercer far than flame.

XII.

" We near'd the wild wood—'twas so wide,
I saw no bounds on either side:
'Twas studded with old sturdy trees,
That bent not to the roughest breeze
Which howls down from Siberia's waste,¹
And strips the forest in its haste,—
But these were few and far between.
Set thick with shrubs more young and green
Luxuriant with their annual leaves,
Ere strown by those autumnal eves
That nip the forest's foliage dead,
Discolor'd with a lifeless red,
Which stands thereon like stiffen'd gore
Upon the slain when battle's o'er,
And some long winter's night hath shed
Its frost o'er every tombless head,
So cold and stark the raven's beak
May peck unpierced each frozen cheek:
'Twas a wild waste of underwood,
And here and there a chestnut stood,

¹ a vast Russian territory in north Asia.

The strong oak, and the hardy pine;
  But far apart—and well it were,
Or else a different lot were mine—
  The boughs gave way, and did not tear
My limbs; and I found strength to bear
My wounds, already scarr'd with cold—
My bonds forbade to loose my hold.
We rustled through the leaves like wind,
Left shrubs, and trees, and wolves behind;
By night I heard them on the track,
Their troop came hard upon our back,
With their long gallop, which can tire
The hound's deep hate, and hunter's fire;
Where'er we flew they follow'd on,
Nor left us with the morning sun;
Behind I saw them, scarce a rood,
At daybreak winding through the wood,
And through the night had heard their feet
Their stealing, rustling step repeat.
Oh! how I wish'd for spear or sword,
At least to die amidst the horde,[1]
And perish—if it must be so—
At bay,[2] destroying many a foe!
When first my courser's race begun,
I wish'd the goal already won;
But now I doubted strength and speed.
Vain doubt! his swift and savage breed
Had nerved him like the mountain-roe:
Nor faster falls the blinding snow
Which whelms the peasant near the door
Whose threshold he shall cross no more,
Bewilder'd with the dazzling blast,
  Than through the forest-paths he pass'd—

---

[1] of wolves.
[2] having no means of escape, and therefore compelled to face the enemy or pursuer, as a stag at bay.

Untired, untamed, and worse than wild;
All furious as a favor'd child
Balk'd of its wish ; or fiercer still—
A woman piqued—who has her will.

XIII.

" The wood was pass'd ; 'twas more than noon,
But chill the air, although in June ;
Or it might be my veins ran cold—
Prolong'd endurance tames the bold;
And I was then not what I seem,
But headlong as a wintry stream,
And wore my feelings out before
I well could count their causes o'er:
And what with fury, fear, and wrath,
The tortures which beset my path,
Cold, hunger, sorrow, shame, distress,
Thus bound in nature's nakedness;
Sprung from a race whose rising blood
When stirr'd beyond its calmer mood,
And trodden hard upon, is like
The rattlesnake's, in act to strike,
What marvel if this worn-out trunk
Beneath its woes a moment sunk ?
The earth gave way, the skies roll'd round,
I seem'd to sink upon the ground;
But err'd, for I was fastly bound.
My heart turn'd sick, my brain grew sore
And throbb'd awhile, then beat no more:
The skies spun like a mighty wheel;
I saw the trees like drunkards reel,
And a slight flash sprang o'er my eyes,
Which saw no farther : he who dies
Can die no more than then I died.
O'ertortured by that ghastly ride,

I felt the blackness come and go,
  And strove to wake ; but could not make
My senses climb up from below:
I felt as on a plank at sea,
When all the waves that dash o'er thee,
At the same time upheave and whelm,
And hurl thee towards a desert realm.
My undulating life was as
The fancied lights that flitting pass
Our shut eyes in deep midnight, when
Fever begins upon the brain;
But soon it pass'd with little pain,
  But a confusion worse than such:
  I own that I should deem it much,
Dying, to feel the same again;
And yet I do suppose we must
Feel far more ere we turn to dust:
No matter ; I have bared my brow
Full in Death's face—before—and now.

XIV.

" My thoughts came back ; where was I ?   Cold
  And numb and giddy : pulse by pulse
Life reassumed its lingering hold,
And throb by throb,—till grown a pang
  Which for a moment would convulse,
  My blood reflow'd, though thick and chill ;
My ear with uncouth noises rang,
  My heart began once more to thrill,
My sight return'd, though dim, alas !
And thicken'd, as it were, with glass.
Methought the dash of waves was nigh;
There was a gleam too of the sky,
Studded with stars ;—it is no dream;
The wild horse swims the wilder stream !

The bright, broad river's gushing tide
Sweeps, winding onward, far and wide,
And we are half-way, struggling o'er
To you unknown and silent shore.
The waters broke my hollow trance,
And with a temporary strength
   My stiffen'd limbs were rebaptized.
My courser's broad breast proudly braves,
And dashes off the ascending waves,
And onward we advance!
We reach the slippery shore at length,
   A haven I but little prized,
For all behind was dark and drear,
And all before was night and fear.
How many hours of night or day
In those suspended pangs I lay,
I could not tell; I scarcely knew
If this were human breath I drew.

XV.

"With glossy skin, and dripping mane,
   And reeling limbs, and reeking flank,
The wild steed's sinewy nerves still strain
   Up the repelling bank.
We gain the top; a boundless plain
Spreads through the shadow of the night,
   And onward, onward, onward, seems,
   Like precipices in our dreams,
To stretch beyond the sight;
And here and there a speck of white,
   Or scatter'd spot of dusky green,
In masses broke into the light,
As rose the moon upon my right:
   But nought distinctly seen
In the dim waste would indicate
The omen of a cottage gate;

No twinkling taper from afar
Stood like a hospitable star;
Not even an ignis-fatuus[1] rose
To make him merry with my woes:
  That very cheat had[2] cheer'd me then:
Although detected, welcome still,
Reminding me, through every ill,
  Of the abodes of men.

XVI.

" Onward we went—but slack and slow;
  His savage force at length o'erspent,
The drooping courser, faint and low,
  All feebly foaming went.
A sickly infant had had power
To guide him forward in that hour;
  But useless all to me :
His new-born tameness nought avail'd—
My limbs were bound ; my force had fail'd,
  Perchance, had they been free.
With feeble effort still I tried
To rend the bonds so starkly tied.
  But still it was in vain;
My limbs were only wrung the more,
And soon the idle strife gave o'er.
  Which but prolong'd their pain:
The dizzy race seem'd almost done,
Although no goal was nearly won:
Some streaks announced the coming sun—
  How slow, alas ! he came !
Methought that mist of dawning gray
Would never dapple into day;
How heavily it roll'd away—
  Before the eastern flame

---

[1] a light that sometimes appears in the night over marshy ground, said to be caused by the decay of animal or vegetable matter—popularly called will-o'-the-wisp.
[2] would have.

Rose crimson, and deposed the stars,
And call'd the radiance from their cars,
And fill'd the earth, from his deep throne,
With lonely lustre, all his own.

XVII.

"Up rose the sun : the mists were curl'd
Back from the solitary world
Which lay around—behind—before
What booted it¹ to traverse o'er
Plain, forest, river ?   Man nor brute,
Nor dint of hoof, nor print of foot,
Lay in the wild luxuriant soil;
No sign of travel—none of toil.
The very air was mute;
And not an insect's shrill small horn,
Nor matin² bird's new voice was borne
From herb nor thicket.   Many a werst,³
Panting as if his heart would burst,
The weary brute still stagger'd on;
And still we were—or seem'd—alone.
At length, while reeling on our way,
Methought I heard a courser neigh,
From out yon tuft of blackening firs.
Is it the wind those branches stirs ?
No, no ! from out the forest prance
     A trampling troop ; I see them come !
In one vast squadron they advance !
     I strove to cry—my lips were dumb.
The steeds rush on in plunging pride;
But where are they the reins to guide ?
A thousand horse—and none to ride !

---
¹ what advantage was it ?
² morning.
³ a Russian measure of distance, somewhat less than three-quarters of a mile.

With flowing tail, and flying mane,
Wide nostrils—never stretch'd by pain,
Mouths bloodless to the bit or rein,
And feet that iron never shod,
And flanks unscarr'd by spur or rod,
A thousand horse, the wild, the free,
Like waves that follow o'er the sea,[1]
   Came thickly thundering on,
As if our faint approach to meet;
The sight renerved my courser's feet,
A moment staggering, feebly fleet,
A moment, with a faint low neigh,
   He answer'd, and then fell;
With gasps and glazing eyes he lay,
   And reeking limbs immovable,
     His first and last career is done!
On came the troop—they saw him stoop,
   They saw me strangely bound along
His back with many a bloody thong:
They stop—they start—they snuff the air,
Gallop a moment here and there,
Approach, retire, wheel round and round,
Then plunging back with sudden bound,
Headed by one black mighty steed,
Who seem'd the patriarch of his breed,
   Without a single speck or hair
Of white upon his shaggy hide;
They snort—they foam—neigh—swerve aside
And backward to the forest fly,
By instinct, from a human eye.
   They left me there to my despair,
Link'd to the dead and stiffening wretch
Whose lifeless limbs beneath me stretch,
Relieved from that unwonted weight,

[1] it was a troop of wild horses.

From whence I could not extricate
Nor him nor me—and there we lay
  The dying on the dead !
I little deem'd another day
  Would see my houseless, helpless head.

" And there from morn till twilight bound,
I felt the heavy hours toil round,
With just enough of life to see
My last of suns go down on me,
In hopeless certainty of mind,
That makes us feel at length resign'd
To that which our foreboding years
Present the worst and last of fears:
Inevitable—even a boon,
Nor more unkind for coming soon,
Yet shunn'd and dreaded with such care,
As if it only were a snare
  That prudence might escape:
At times both wish'd for and implored,
At times sought with self-pointed sword,
Yet still a dark and hideous close
To even intolerable woes,
  And welcome in no shape.
And, strange to say, the sons of pleasure,
They who have revell'd beyond measure
In beauty, wassail, wine, and treasure,
Die calm, and calmer, oft than he
Whose heritage was misery:
For he who hath in turn run through
All that was beautiful and new,
  Hath nought to hope, and nought to leave;
And, save the future (which is view'd
Not quite as men are base or good,
But as their nerves may be endued),

With nought perhaps to grieve:
The wretch still hopes his woes must end,
And Death, whom he should deem his friend,
Appears, to his distemper'd eyes,
Arrived to rob him of his prize,
The tree of his new Paradise.
To-morrow would have given him all,
Repaid his pangs, repair'd his fall;
To-morrow would have been the first
Of days no more deplored or curst.
But bright, and long, and beckoning years,
Seen dazzling through the mist of tears,
Guerdon of many a painful hour;
To-morrow would have given him power
To rule, to shine, to smite, to save—
And must it dawn upon his grave?

XVIII.

"The sun was sinking—still I lay
  Chain'd to the chill and stiffening steed;
I thought to mingle there our clay;
  And my dim eyes of death had need,
  No hope arose of being freed:
I cast my last looks up the sky,
  And there between me and the sun
I saw the expecting raven fly,
Who scarce would wait till both should die,
  Ere his repast begun;
He flew, and perch'd, then flew once more,
And each time nearer than before;
I saw his wing through twilight flit,
And once so near me he alit,
  I could have smote, but lack'd the strength;
But the slight motion of my hand,
And feeble scratching of the sand,

The exerted throat's faint struggling noise
Which scarcely could be call'd a voice,
  Together scared him off at length.
I know no more—my latest dream
  Is something of a lovely star
  Which fix'd my dull eyes from afar,
And went and came with wandering beam,
And of the cold, dull, swimming, dense
  Sensation of recurring sense,
And then subsiding back to death,
And then again a little breath,
A little thrill, a short suspense,
An icy sickness curdling o'er
My heart, and sparks that cross'd my brain,
A gasp, a throb, a start of pain,
A sigh, and nothing more.

XIX.

"I woke—Where was I?—Do I see
A human face look down on me?
And doth a roof above me close?
Do these limbs on a couch repose?
Is this a chamber where I lie?
And is it mortal yon bright eye
That watches me with gentle glance?
  I closed my own again once more,
As doubtful that my former trance
  Could not as yet be o'er.
A slender girl, long hair'd, and tall,
Sate watching by the cottage wall;
The sparkle of her eye I caught,
Even with my first return of thought;
For ever and anon¹ she threw
  A prying, pitying glance on me
  With her black eyes so wild and free:

¹ now and then.

I gazed, and gazed, until I knew
  No vision it could be,—
But that I lived and was released
From adding to the vulture's feast:
And when the Cossack maid beheld
My heavy eyes at length unseal'd,
She smiled—and I essay'd to speak,
  But fail'd—and she approach'd, and made
  With lip and finger signs that said,
I must not strive as yet to break
The silence, till my strength should be
Enough to leave my accents free;
And then her hand on mine she laid,
And smooth'd the pillow for my head,
And stole along on tiptoe tread,
  And gently oped the door, and spake
In whispers—ne'er was voice so sweet!
Even music follow'd her light feet;
  But those she call'd were not awake,
And she went forth; but, ere she pass'd,
Another look on me she cast,
  Another sign she made, to say,
That I had naught to fear, that all
Were near, at my command or call,
  And she would not delay
Her due return:—while she was gone,
Methought I felt too much alone.

XX.

"She came with mother and with sire—
What need of more?—I will not tire
With long recital of the rest,
Since I became the Cossack's guest.
They found me senseless on the plain—
  They bore me to the nearest hut—

They brought me into life again—
Me—one day o'er their realm to reign !
  Thus the vain fool who strove to glut
His rage, refining on my pain,
    Sent me forth to the wilderness,
Bound, naked, bleeding, and alone,
To pass the desert to a throne,—
  What mortal his own doom may guess ?
  Let none despond, let none despair !
To-morrow the Borysthenes
May see our coursers gaze at ease
Upon his Turkish bank,—and never
Had I such welcome for a river
  As I shall yield when safely there.
Comrades, good night !"—The Hetman threw
  His length beneath the oak-tree shade,
  With leafy couch already made,
A bed nor comfortless nor new
To him, who took his rest whene'er
The hour arrived, no matter where:
  His eyes the hastening slumbers steep.
And if ye marvel Charles forgot
To thank his tale, *he* wondered not,—
  The king had been an hour asleep.

CHILDE[1] HAROLD.

This poem describes scenes and events in several parts of Europe, in which the poet travelled—Portugal and Spain, Greece and neighboring lands, Belgium, Germany and the Rhine country, Switzerland and Italy.

It was thought by some that Childe Harold was meant to represent the author himself. This, however, Byron denied. In the preface to the first and second cantos he says:—

"A fictitious character is introduced for the sake of giving some connection to the piece. It has been suggested to me by friends, that in this fictitious character, 'Childe Harold,' I may incur the suspicion of having intended some real personage; this I beg leave to disclaim. Harold is the child of imagination. In some very trivial particulars, and those merely local, there might be grounds for such a notion, but in the main points none whatever."

But while Childe Harold is an imaginary character, the spirit and sentiment of the poem are the author's. Its beautiful pictures are presented to us as Byron saw them. He tells us what he thought and how he felt in relation to all that came under his observation, and he tells it in a way that all through interests and delights the reader.

CANTO[2] THE FIRST.

I.

OH, thou, in Hellas[3] deemed of heavenly birth,
Muse,[4] formed or fabled at the minstrel's will !
Since shamed full oft by later lyres on earth,
Mine dares not call thee from thy sacred hill :[5]
Yet there I've wandered by thy vaunted rill ;[6]
Yes ! sighed o'er Delphi's long-deserted shrine,[7]
Where, save that feeble fountain,[6] all is still ;
Nor mote[8] my shell[9] awake the weary Nine[4]
To grace so plain a tale—this lowly lay[10] of mine.

---

[1] In former times this word was used as a prefix to the name of the eldest son until he succeeded to the title of the family.

[2] part or division of a long poem.   [3] ancient name of Greece.

[4] In the ancient Greek mythology there were nine goddesses, who presided over poetry, music, and the sciences. They were called the Nine Muses. The muse here referred to is the goddess of poetry.

[5] the hill or mount of Parnassus in Greece, on the top of which the Muses were supposed to hold their meetings.

[6] the rill or fountain of Castalia, on the slope of Mount Parnassus. It was thought that those who drank of its waters received the gift of poetry.

[7] an altar or sacred place. Delphi (now Castri) was a town at the foot of Parnassus, where there was a temple of Apollo, the god of music, poetry, and the fine arts.

[8] might.

[9] musical instrument or lyre, the first, it is said, being made by strings drawn over a tortoise-shell.   [10] song.

II.

Whilom¹ in Albion's² isle there dwelt a youth,
Who ne³ in virtue's ways did take delight;
But spent his days in riot most uncouth,
And vexed with mirth the drowsy ear of Night.

. . . . . .

III.

Childe Harold was he hight;⁴ but whence his name
And lineage long, it suits me not to say:
Suffice it, that perchance they were of fame,
And had been glorious in another day:
But one sad losel⁵ soils a name for aye,⁶
However mighty in the olden time;
Nor all that heralds⁷ rake from coffined clay,
Nor florid prose, nor honeyed lines of rhyme,
Can blazon evil deeds, or consecrate a crime.

IV.

Childe Harold basked him in the noontide sun,
Disporting there like any other fly,
Nor deemed before his little day was done
One blast might chill him into misery.
But long ere scarce a third of his passed by,
Worse than adversity the Childe befell:
He felt the fullness of satiety:
Then loathed he in his native land to dwell,
Which seemed to him more lone than eremite's⁸ sad cell.

. . . . . .

VII.

The Childe departed from his father's hall;
It was a vast and venerable pile;

---

¹ formerly. ² Albion, ancient name of Great Britain. ³ not
⁴ called. ⁵ worthless person. ⁶ (*pron.* ā) ever.
⁷ herald, an official who traces and draws up records of the founders or ancestors of families. ⁸ hermit's.

So old, it seemed only not to fall,
Yet strength was pillared in each massy aisle.

. . . . . .

X.

Childe Harold had a mother—not forgot,
Though parting from that mother he did shun ;
A sister whom he loved, but saw her not
Before his weary pilgrimage begun :
If friends he had, he bade adieu to none.
Yet deem not thence his breast a breast of steel :
Ye, who have known what 'tis to dote upon
A few dear objects, will in sadness feel
Such partings break the heart they fondly hope to heal.

. . . . . .

XII.

The sails were filled, and the fair light winds blew
As glad to waft him from his native home ;
And fast the white rocks faded from his view,
And soon were lost in circumambient [1] foam :
And then, it may be, of his wish to roam
Repented he, but in his bosom slept
The silent thought, nor from his lips did come
One word of wail, whilst others sate and wept,
And to the reckless gales unmanly moaning kept.

XIII.

But when the sun was sinking in the sea,
He seized his harp, which he at times could string,
And strike, albeit with untaught melody,
When deemed he no strange ear was listening :
And now his fingers o'er it he did fling,
And tuned his farewell in the dim twilight,
While flew the vessel on her snowy wing,

[1] surrounding.

And fleeting shores receded from his sight,
Thus to the elements¹ he poured his last " Good Night."

Adieu, adieu ! my native shore
  Fades o'er the waters blue ;
The night-winds sigh, the breakers roar,
  And shrieks the wild sea-mew.
Yon sun that sets upon the sea
  We follow in his flight ;
Farewell awhile to him and thee,
  My Native Land—Good Night !

A few short hours, and he will rise
  To give the morrow birth ;
And I shall hail the main and skies,
  But not my mother earth.
Deserted is my own good hall,
  Its hearth is desolate ;
Wild weeds are gathering on the wall,
  My dog howls at the gate.

" Come hither, hither, my little page ;
  Why dost thou weep and wail ?
Or dost thou dread the billow's rage,
  Or tremble at the gale ?
But dash the tear-drop from thine eye,
  Our ship is swift and strong ;
Our fleetest falcon scarce can fly
  More merrily along."

" Let winds be shrill, let waves roll high,
  I fear not wave nor wind ;
Yet marvel not, Sir Childe, that I
  Am sorrowful in mind.

¹ here meaning the air and ocean.

For I have from my father gone,
  A mother whom I love,
And have no friend, save thee alone,
  But thee—and One above.

" My father blessed me fervently,
  Yet did not much complain ;
But sorely will my mother sigh
  Till I come back again."—
" Enough, enough, my little lad !
  Such tears become thine eye ;
If I thy guileless bosom had,
  Mine own would not be dry."

  .   .   .   .   .   .

With thee, my bark, I'll swiftly go
  Athwart the foaming brine ;
Nor care what land thou bear'st me to,
  So not again to mine.
Welcome, welcome, ye dark blue waves !
  And when you fail my sight,
Welcome, ye deserts, and ye caves !
  My Native Land—Good Night !

XIV.

On, on the vessel flies, the land is gone,
And winds are rude in Biscay's sleepless bay.
Four days are sped, but with the fifth, anon,
New shores descried make every bosom gay ;
And Cintra's[1] mountain greets them on their way,
And Tagus[2] dashing onward to the deep,
His fabled golden tribute [3] bent to pay ;

---

[1] Cintra, a town on the side of a mountain near Lisbon in Portugal.
[2] a river that flows through Spain and Portugal into the Atlantic at Lisbon.
[3] it was said in ancient times that the sands of the Tagus produced gold and precious stones.

And soon on board the Lusian¹ pilots leap,
And steer 'twixt fertile shores where yet few rustics reap.

. . . .

XVI.

What beauties doth Lisboa² first unfold!
Her image floating on that noble tide,
Which poets vainly pave with sands of gold,
But now whereon a thousand keels did ride
Of mighty strength, since Albion was allied,
And to the Lusians did her aid afford:³
A nation swoll'n with ignorance and pride,⁴
Who lick, yet loathe, the hand that waves the sword.
To save them from the wrath of Gaul's unsparing lord.

XVII.

But whoso entereth within this town,
That, sheening⁵ far, celestial seems to be,
Disconsolate will wander up and down,
Mid many things unsightly to strange e'e;⁶
For hut and palace show like filthily;
The dingy denizens⁷ are reared in dirt;
Ne personage of high or mean degree
Doth care for cleanness of surtout or shirt,
Though shent⁸ with Egypt's plague, unkempt, unwashed, unhurt.

XVIII.

Poor, paltry slaves! yet born midst noblest scenes—
Why, Nature, waste thy wonders on such men?

---

¹ Lusitania was the ancient name of Portugal.
² Portuguese name of Lisbon.
³ in 1807 Napoleon Bonaparte seized Portugal. This caused the Peninsular War, in which the English, Portuguese, and Spaniards fought against the French.
⁴ the Lusians are represented as ignorant and proud, fawning upon, while they loathe, the hand of England, whose aid they receive to save them from the wrath of Napoleon, the lord of France (Gaul).
⁵ shining.　　⁶ eye.　　⁷ inhabitants.　　⁸ degraded.

Lo! Cintra's glorious Eden [1] intervenes
In variegated maze of mount and glen.
Ah me! what hand can pencil guide, or pen,
To follow half on which the eye dilates
Through views more dazzling unto mortal ken [2]
Than those whereof such things the bard relates,
Who to the awe-struck world unlocked Elysium's [3] gates?

XIX.

The horrid crags, by toppling [4] convent crowned,
The cork-trees hoar that clothe the shaggy steep,
The mountain moss by scorching skies imbrowned.
The sunken glen, whose sunless shrubs must weep,
The tender azure of the unruffled deep,
The orange tints that gild the greenest bough,
The torrents that from cliff to valley leap,
The vine on high, the willow branch below,
Mixed in one mighty scene, with varied beauty glow.

. . . .

XXI.

And here and there, as up the crags you spring,
Mark many rude-carved crosses near the path :
Yet deem not these devotion's offering—
These are memorials frail of murderous wrath ;
For wheresoe'er the shrieking victim hath
Poured forth his blood beneath the assassin's knife,
Some hand erects a cross of moldering lath ;
And grove and glen with thousand such are rife
Throughout this purple land, where law secures not life. [5]

. . . .

[1] beautiful gardens around Cintra.   [2] view.
[3] Elysium was the Greek paradise. or abode of the blessed dead.
[4] on the top of high rocks, as if in danger of falling over.
[5] in 1809, about the time at which the poet wrote, murders were very frequent in the streets of Lisbon and its vicinity.

XXX.

O'er vales that teem with fruits, romantic hills.
(Oh that such hills upheld a free-born race!)
Whereon to gaze the eye with joyance fills,
Childe Harold wends through many a pleasant place,
Though sluggards deem it but a foolish chase,
And marvel men should quit their easy chair,
The toilsome way, and long, long league to trace.
Oh, there is sweetness in the mountain air
And life, that bloated Ease [1] can never hope to share.

XXXI.

More bleak to view the hills at length recede,
And less luxuriant, smoother vales extend :
Immense horizon-bounded plains succeed !
Far as the eye discerns, withouten [2] end,
Spain's realms appear, whereon her shepherds tend
Flocks, whose rich fleece right well the trader knows—
Now must the pastor's arms his lambs defend :
For Spain is compassed by unyielding foes, [3]
And all must shield their all, or share Subjection's woes.

. . . . . .

XXXVII.

Awake, ye sons of Spain ! awake ! advance.
Lo ! Chivalry, [4] your ancient goddess, cries,
But wields not, as of old, her thirsty lance,
Nor shakes her crimson plumage in the skies :
Now on the smoke of blazing bolts [5] she flies,
And speaks in thunder through yon engine's roar !
In every peal she calls—" Awake ! arise ! "

---

[1] ease is here personified, or imagined as being a living person ; hence the capital letter. Such figurative use of words is frequent throughout the poem.
[2] old form of without.   [3] the French.
[4] knighthood ; the gallantry and courtesy of the knights of the middle ages.
[5] artillery ; cannon shots.

Say, is her voice more feeble than of yore,
When her war-song was heard on Andalusia's[1] shore?

. . . . . .

XLIII.

O Albuera,[2] glorious field of grief!
As o'er thy plain the Pilgrim pricked his steed,
Who could foresee thee, in a space so brief,
A scene where mingling foes should boast and bleed.
Peace to the perished! may the warrior's meed
And tears of triumph their reward prolong!
Till others fall where other chieftains lead,
Thy name shall circle round the gaping throng,
And shine in worthless lays, the theme of transient song.

. . . . . .

XLV.

Full swiftly Harold wends his lonely way
Where proud Sevilla[3] triumphs unsubdued:
Yet is she free—the spoiler's wished-for prey!
Soon, soon shall Conquest's fiery foot intrude,
Blackening her lovely domes with traces rude.
Inevitable hour! 'Gainst fate to strive
Where Desolation plants her famished brood
Is vain, or Ilion,[4] Tyre,[5] might yet survive,
And Virtue vanquish all, and Murder[6] cease to thrive.

XLVI.

But all unconscious of the coming doom,[7]
The feast, the song, the revel here abounds;

---

[1] a province in the south of Spain.
[2] a village of Spain, where in 1811 a great battle was fought between the English, Spanish, and Portuguese forces and the French, in which the latter were defeated.
[3] Seville, a famous and beautiful city of Spain.
[4] another name of the ancient city of Troy, which was destroyed by the Greeks in the famous Trojan war. [5] an ancient city of Phœnicia in Asia Minor.
[6] Murder, Virtue, Desolation, as well as War and Love in the following stanza, are all personifications.
[7] the taking and ravaging of Seville in 1810 by the French General Soult.

Strange modes of merriment the hours consume,
Nor bleed these patriots with their country's wounds;
Nor here War's clarion, but Love's rebeck ¹ sounds;
. . . . . .

XLIX.

On yon long level plain, at distance crowned
With crags, whereon those Moorish ² turrets rest,
Wide scattered hoof-marks dint the wounded ground;
And, scathed by fire, the greensward's darkened vest
Tells that the foe was Andalusia's guest:³
Here was the camp, the watch-flame, and the host,
Here the brave peasant stormed the dragon's nest:⁴
Still does he mark it with triumphant boast,
And points to yonder cliffs, which oft were won and lost.

L.

And whomsoe'er along the path you meet
Bears in his cap the badge of crimson hue,⁵
Which tells you whom to shun and whom to greet.
Woe to the man that walks in public view
Without of loyalty this token true:
Sharp is the knife, and sudden is the stroke:
And sorely would the Gallic⁶ foeman rue,
If subtle poniards, wrapt beneath the cloak,
Could blunt the saber's edge, or clear the cannon's smoke.

LI.

At every turn Morena's ⁷ dusky height
Sustains aloft the battery's iron load;

---

¹ a kind of fiddle with two strings.
² Spain was invaded and conquered in the eighth century by the Arabs, and later by the Moors, who long remained masters of the country.
³ in 1810 Andalusia (province of Spain) was seized and occupied by the French.
⁴ the Spanish peasants fought bravely to drive out the French invaders.
⁵ the red cockade, bearing in its centre a likeness of the Spanish King Ferdinand VII.
⁶ French.   ⁷ Morena, a mountain in the south of Spain.

And, far as mortal eye can compass sight,
The mountain howitzer,¹ the broken road,
The bristling palisade, the fosse o'erflowed,
The stationed bands, the never-vacant watch,
The magazine in rocky durance stowed,
The holstered steed beneath the shed of thatch,
The ball-piled pyramid,² the ever-blazing match,

LII.

Portend the deeds to come : but he³ whose nod
Has tumbled feebler despots from their sway,
A moment pauseth ere he lifts the rod ;
A little moment deigneth to delay :
Soon will his legions sweep through these their way ;
The West must own the Scourger³ of the world.
Ah, Spain ! how sad will be thy reckoning day,
When soars Gaul's Vulture,³ with his wings unfurled,
And thou shalt view thy sons in crowds to Hades⁴ hurled.

LIII.

And must they fall—the young, the proud, the brave—
To swell one bloated chief's³ unwholesome reign ?
No step between submission and a grave ?
The rise of rapine and the fall of Spain ?
And doth the Power that man adores ordain
Their doom, nor heed the suppliant's appeal ?
Is all that desperate Valor acts in vain ?
And Counsel sage, and patriotic Zeal,
The veteran's skill, youth's fire, and manhood's heart of steel ?

LIV.

Is it for this the Spanish maid,⁵ aroused,
Hangs on the willow her unstrung guitar,

¹ a short cannon.
² shot and shells in military forts are piled in heaps shaped like a pyramid.
³ Napoleon.
⁴ the invisible abode of the souls of the dead ; so called by the ancient Greeks.
⁵ Augustina—known as the Maid of Saragoza—a heroic young Spanish woman, who, at the siege of Saragoza (North Spain) in 1809, worked with her countrymen on the batteries, in defending the town against the French.

And, all unsexed, the anlace¹ hath espoused,
Sung the loud song, and dared the deed of war?
And she, whom once the semblance of a scar
Appalled, an owlet's larum² chilled with dread,
Now views the column-scattering bayonet jar,
The falchion flash, and o'er the yet warm dead
Stalks with Minerva's³ step where Mars⁴ might quake to tread.

LV.

Ye who shall marvel when you hear her tale,
Oh! had you known her in her softer hour,
Marked her black eye that mocks her coal-black veil,
Heard her light, lively tones in Lady's bower,
Seen her long locks that foil the painter's power,
Her fairy form, with more than female grace,
Scarce would you deem that Saragoza's tower
Beheld her smile in Danger's Gorgon⁵ face,
Thin the closed ranks, and lead in Glory's fearful chase.

LVI.

Her lover sinks—she sheds no ill-timed tear;
Her chief is slain—she fills his fatal post;
Her fellows flee—she checks their base career;
The foe retires—she heads the sallying host:
Who can appease like her a lover's ghost?
Who can avenge so well a leader's fall?
What maid retrieve when man's flushed hope is lost?
Who hang so fiercely on the flying Gaul,
Foiled by a woman's hand, before a battered wall?

LVII.

Yet are Spain's maids no race of Amazons,⁶
But formed for all the witching arts of love:

---

¹ a short dagger. ² alarm; a noise giving notice of danger.
³ Minerva, worshipped by the ancients as the goddess of wisdom and war.
⁴ the god of war.
⁵ of frightful appearance; like the Gorgons, fabled monsters so terrible to behold that anyone who looked upon their faces was immediately turned into stone.
⁶ a nation of female warriors, supposed, in ancient times, to have dwelt on the shores of the Black Sea.

Though thus in arms they emulate her sons,
And in the horrid phalanx dare to move,
'Tis but the tender fierceness of the dove,
Pecking the hand that hovers o'er her mate :
In softness as in firmness far above
Remoter females,¹ famed for sickening prate :
Her mind is nobler sure, her charms perchance as great.

. . . .

LX.

O thou, Parnassus ! whom I now survey,²
Not in the phrenzy of a dreamer's eye,
Not in the fabled landscape of a lay,
But soaring snow-clad through thy native sky,
In the wild pomp of mountain majesty !
What marvel if I thus essay to sing ?
The humblest of thy pilgrims passing by
Would gladly woo thine echoes with his string,³
Though from thy heights no more one Muse will wave her wing.

LXI.

Oft have I dreamed of Thee! whose glorious name
Who knows not, knows not man's divinest lore :⁴
And now I view thee, 'tis, alas, with shame
That I in feeblest accents must adore.
When I recount thy worshipers of yore⁵
I tremble, and can only bend the knee ;
Nor raise my voice, nor vainly dare to soar,
But gaze beneath thy cloudy canopy
In silent joy to think at last I look on thee !

LXII.

Happier in this than mightiest bards have been,
Whose fate to distant homes confined their lot,

¹ referring to the ladies of England.
² This part of the poem was written in Greece (see note 5, page 45).
³ his lyre.   ⁴ knowledge.   ⁵ ancient times.

Shall I unmoved behold the hallowed scene,
Which others rave of, though they know it not?
Though here no more Apollo haunts his grot,[1]
And thou, the Muses' seat, art now their grave,
Some gentle spirit still pervades the spot,
Sighs in the gale, keeps silence in the cave,
And glides with glassy foot o'er yon melodious wave.

LXIII.

Of thee hereafter.—Even amidst my strain[2]
I turned aside to pay my homage here;
Forgot the land, the sons, the maids of Spain;
Her fate, to every freeborn bosom dear;
And hailed thee, not perchance without a tear.
Now to my theme—but from thy holy haunt
Let me some remnant, some memorial bear;
Yield me one leaf of Daphne's deathless plant,[3]
Nor let thy votary's hope be deemed an idle vaunt.

LXIV.

But ne'er didst thou, fair Mount, when Greece was young.
See round thy giant base a brighter choir;
Nor e'er did Delphi, when her priestess sung
The Pythian[4] hymn with more than mortal fire,
Behold a train more fitting to inspire
The song of love than Andalusia's maids,
Nurst in the glowing lap of soft desire:
Ah! that to these were given such peaceful shades
As Greece can still bestow, though Glory fly her glades.

LXV.

Fair is proud Seville; let her country boast
Her strength, her wealth, her site of ancient days,

---

[1] see note 6, page 45. [2] poem; song.
[3] the laurel; Daphne, a beautiful nymph loved by Apollo, and changed into a laurel tree.
[4] Pythia, name given to the priestess who served in the temple of Apollo at Delphi.

But Cadiz,[1] rising on the distant coast,
Calls forth a sweeter, though ignoble praise.
. . . . .

LXVIII.

The Sabbath comes, a day of blessed rest ;
What hallows it upon this Christian shore ?
Lo! it is sacred to a solemn feast :
Hark! heard you not the forest monarch's[2] roar ?
Crashing the lance, he snuffs the spouting gore
Of man and steed, o'erthrown beneath his horn :
The thronged arena shakes with shouts for more :
Yells the mad crowd o'er entrails freshly torn.
Nor shrinks the female eye, nor e'en affects to mourn.

LXIX.

The seventh day this : the jubilee of man.
London! right well thou know'st the day of prayer :
Then thy spruce citizen, washed artisan,
And smug apprentice gulp their weekly air :
. . . . . .
To Hampstead, Brentford, Harrow,[3] make repair :
. . . . . .

LXX.

Some o'er thy Thamis[4] row the ribboned fair,
Others along the safer turnpike fly,
Some Richmond Hill[5] ascend, some scud to Ware,[3]
And many to the steep of Highgate[6] hie.
. . . .

LXXI.

All have their fooleries ; not alike are thine,
Fair Cadiz, rising o'er the dark-blue sea !

---

[1] town on the southwestern coast of Spain.
[2] forest monarch, the bull. The poet goes on to describe a Spanish bull-fight.
[3] towns near London, England. [4] the river Thames, which flows through London.
[5] new London. [6] a suburb of London.

Soon as the matin[1] bell proclaimeth nine,
Thy saint adorers count the rosary:[2]

. . . .

Then to the crowded circus forth they fare:
Young, old, high, low, at once the same diversion share.

LXXII.

The lists are oped, the spacious area cleared,
Thousands on thousands piled are seated round;
Long ere the first loud trumpet's note is heard,
No vacant space for lated wight[3] is found:

. . . .

LXXIII.

Hushed is the din of tongues—on gallant steeds,
With milk-white crest, gold spur, and light-poised lance,
Four cavaliers prepare for venturous deeds,
And lowly bending to the lists advance;
Rich are their scarfs, their chargers featly[4] prance:
If in the dangerous game they shine to-day,
The crowd's loud shout, and ladies' lovely glance,
Best prize of better acts, they bear away,
And all that kings or chiefs e'er gain their toils repay.

LXXIV.

In costly sheen[5] and gaudy cloak arrayed,
But all afoot, the light-limbed Matadore[6]
Stands in the center, eager to invade
The lord of lowing herds; but not before
The ground, with cautious tread, is traversed o'er,
Lest aught unseen should lurk to thwart his speed:
His arms a dart, he fights aloof, nor more

---

[1] morning.
[2] a string of beads for counting prayers.
[3] a belated person can find no seat.
[4] neatly; dexterously.
[5] splendor.
[6] the man appointed to kill the bull in a bull-fight.

Can man achieve without the friendly steed—
Alas! too oft condemned for him to bear and bleed.

LXXV.

Thrice sounds the clarion ; lo ! the signal falls,
The den expands, and Expectation mute
Gapes round the silent circle's peopled walls.
Bounds with one lashing spring the mighty brute,
And wildly staring, spurns, with sounding foot,
The sand, nor blindly rushes on his foe :
Here, there, he points his threatening front, to suit
His first attack, wide waving to and fro
His angry tail ; red rolls his eye's dilated glow.

LXXVI.

Sudden he stops ; his eye is fixed : away,
Away, thou heedless boy ! prepare the spear ;
Now is thy time to perish, or display
The skill that yet may check his mad career.
With well-timed croupe¹ the nimble coursers veer ;
On foams the bull, but not unscathed he goes ;
Streams from his flank the crimson torrent clear
He flies, he wheels, distracted with his throes :
Dart follows dart ; lance, lance ; loud bellowings speak
his woes.

LXXVII.

Again he comes ; nor dart nor lance avail,
Nor the wild plunging of the tortured horse ;
Though man and man's avenging arms assail,
Vain are his weapons, vainer is his force.
One gallant steed is stretched a mangled corse ;
Another, hideous sight ! unseamed appears.
His gory chest unveils life's panting source ;
Though death-struck, still his feeble frame he rears :
Staggering, but stemming all, his lord unharmed he bears.

¹ leap.

LXXVIII.

Foiled, bleeding, breathless, furious to the last,
Full in the center stands the bull at bay,
'Mid wounds, and clinging darts, and lances brast,[1]
And foes disabled in the brutal fray :
And now the Matadores around him play,
Shake the red cloak, and poise the ready brand :
Once more through all he bursts his thundering way—
Vain rage ! the mantle quits the conynge[2] hand.
Wraps his fierce eye—'tis past—he sinks upon the sand.

LXXIX.

Where his vast neck just mingles with the spine,
Sheathed in his form the deadly weapon lies.
He stops—he starts—disdaining to decline.
Slowly he falls amidst triumphant cries,
Without a groan, without a struggle dies.
The decorated car appears—on high
The corse is piled—sweet sight for vulgar eyes ;
Four steeds that spurn the rein, as swift as shy,
Hurl the dark bull along, scarce seen in dashing by.

LXXX.

Such the ungentle sport that oft invites
The Spanish maid, and cheers the Spanish swain :
Nurtured in blood betimes, his heart delights
In vengeance, gloating on another's pain.
What private feuds the troubled village stain
Though now one phalanxed host should meet the foe,[3]
Enough, alas, in humble homes remain,
To meditate 'gainst friends the secret blow,
For some slight cause of wrath, whence life's warm stream must flow.

. . . . .

[1] burst ; broken.   [2] cunning.   [3] the French.

LXXXV.

Adieu, fair Cadiz! yea, a long adieu!
Who may forget how well thy walls have stood?
When all were changing, thou alone wert true,
First to be free, and last to be subdued.
And if amidst a scene, a shock so rude,
Some native blood was seen thy streets to dye,
A traitor[1] only fell beneath the feud:
Here all were noble, save nobility;[2]
None hugged a conqueror's chain save fallen Chivalry!

LXXXVI.

Such be the sons of Spain, and strange her fate!
They fight for freedom, who were never free;
A kingless[3] people for a nerveless state.
Her vassals combat when their chieftains flee.
True to the veriest slaves of Treachery;
Fond of a land which gave them naught but life.
Pride points the path that leads to Liberty;
Back to the struggle, baffled in the strife,
War, war is still the cry, " War even to the knife!"[4]

LXXXVII.

Ye, who would more of Spain and Spaniards know,
Go, read whate'er is writ of bloodiest strife:
Whate'er keen Vengeance urged on foreign foe
Can act, is acting there against man's life:
From flashing scimitar to secret knife,
War moldeth there each weapon to his need—
So may he guard the sister and the wife,
So may he make each curst oppressor bleed,
So may such foes deserve the most remorseless deed!

---

[1] Solano, Governor of Cadiz, who was secretly in sympathy with the French, and was killed as a traitor by the people of the town in 1809.
[2] some of the Spanish nobility were in sympathy with the French.
[3] the King of Spain, Charles IV., was compelled by Napoleon to resign the crown.
[4] the answer of the Spanish General Palafox, to the French when they asked him to surrender Saragoza during the siege of that town in 1808.

LXXXVIII.

Flows there a tear of pity for the dead ?
Look o'er the ravage of the reeking plain :
Look on the hands with female slaughter red ;
Then to the dogs resign the unburied slain,
Then to the vulture let each corse remain ;
Albeit unworthy of the prey-bird's maw,
Let their bleached bones, and blood's unbleaching stain,
Long mark the battle-field with hideous awe :
Thus only may our sons conceive the scenes we saw !

LXXXIX.

Nor yet, alas, the dreadful work is done ;
Fresh legions¹ pour adown the Pyrenees :²
It deepens still, the work is scarce begun,
Nor mortal eyes the distant end foresees.
Fall'n nations gaze on Spain : if freed, she frees,
More than her fell³ Pizarros⁴ once enchained.
Strange retribution ! now Columbia's case
Repairs the wrongs that Quito's⁵ sons sustained,
While o'er the parent clime⁶ prowls Murder unrestrained.

XC.

Not all the blood at Talavera shed,
Not all the marvels of Barossa's fight,⁸
Not Albuera⁹ lavish of the dead,
Have won for Spain her well-asserted right.

¹ of the French. ² the mountains between France and Spain. ³ cruel.
⁴ referring to the Spaniard Pizarro, who conquered and plundered Peru in the 16th century.
⁵ Quito, in South America, conquered by the Spaniards.
⁶ Spain.
⁷ a town of Spain, at which the English and Spaniards defeated the French in a great battle, July 27 and 28, 1809.
⁸ at Barossa, a village of Spain, a small number of English defeated a French army in March, 1811.
⁹ see note 1, page 53.

When shall her Olive-Branch be free from blight?
When shall she breathe her from the blushing toil?
How many a doubtful day shall sink in night,
Ere the Frank¹ robber turn him from his spoil,
And Freedom's stranger-tree grow native of the soil?

. . . .

XCIII.

Here is one fytte² of Harold's pilgrimage.
Ye who of him may further seek to know,
Shall find some tidings in a future page,
If he that rhymeth now may scribble more.
Is this too much? Stern critic, say not so;
Patience! and ye shall hear what he beheld
In other lands, where he was doomed to go:
Lands that contain the monuments of Eld,³
Ere Greece and Grecian arts by barbarous hands were
 quelled.

CANTO THE SECOND.

I.

COME, blue-eyed maid of heaven!⁴—but thou, alas,
Didst never yet one mortal song inspire—
Goddess of Wisdom! here⁵ thy temple was,
And is, despite of war and wasting fire,
And years, that bade thy worship to expire:
But worse than steel, and flame, and ages slow,
Is the drear scepter and dominion dire
Of men who never felt the sacred glow
That thoughts of thee and thine on polished breasts be-
 stow.

---

¹ French. ² canto. ³ olden times; antiquity.
⁴ Pallas, goddess of wisdom, named Minerva by the Romans.
⁵ at Athens, of which Pallas was the patron goddess.

5

II.

Ancient of days! august Athena!¹ where,
Where are thy men of might, thy grand in soul?
Gone—glimmering through the dream of things that
   were:
First in the race that led to Glory's goal,
They won, and passed away—is this the whole?
A school-boy's tale, the wonder of an hour!
The warrior's weapon and the sophist's² stole³
Are sought in vain, and o'er each moldering tower,
Dim with the mist of years, gray flits the shade of power.

. . . . . .

X.

Here let me sit upon this massy stone,
The marble column's yet unshaken base!
Here, son of Saturn,⁴ was thy fav'rite throne!⁵
Mightiest of many such! Hence let me trace
The latent grandeur of thy dwelling-place.
It may not be: nor even can Fancy's eye
Restore what time hath labored to deface.
Yet these proud pillars claim no passing sigh;
Unmoved the Moslem⁶ sits, the light Greek carols by.⁷

XI.

But who, of all the plunderers of yon fane
On high, where Pallas lingered, loath to flee
The latest relic of her ancient reign—
The last, the worst, dull spoiler, who was he?

---

¹ Athens, capital of Greece.   ² sophists, public teachers in ancient Greece.
³ a loose dress reaching to the feet.
⁴ king of the gods. Jupiter was his son and successor.
⁵ there was a magnificent temple of Jupiter in Athens.
⁶ believer in the religion of Mohammed.
⁷ meaning that the Moslem and Greek inhabitants of Athens pass by the ruins of the ancient temples and monuments of the city without interest or appreciation.

CHILDE HAROLD.

Blush, Caledonia![1] such thy son[2] could be!
England! I joy no child he was of thine:
Thy free-born men should spare what once was free;
Yet they could violate each saddening shrine,
And bear these altars o'er the long reluctant brine.[3]

. . . . . .

XV.

Cold is the heart, fair Greece, that looks on thee,
Nor feels as lovers o'er the dust they loved;
Dull is the eye that will not weep to see
Thy walls defaced, thy moldering shrines removed
By British hands, which it had best behoved
To guard those relics ne'er to be restored.
Curst be the hour when from their isle they roved,
And once again thy hapless bosom gored,
And snatched thy shrinking Gods to northern climes
  abhorred!

XVI.

But where is Harold? shall I then forget
To urge the gloomy wanderer o'er the wave?
Little recked he of all that men regret;
No loved one now in feigned lament could rave;
No friend the parting hand extended gave,
Ere the cold stranger passed to other climes.
Hard is his heart whom charms may not enslave;
But Harold felt not as in other times,
And left without a sigh the land of war and crimes.

XVII.

He that has sailed upon the dark blue sea,
Has viewed at times, I ween, a full fair sight;

[1] ancient name of Scotland.
[2] the Earl of Elgin, a Scotch nobleman, who carried away from the temple of Minerva in Athens a number of ancient sculptures, now in the British Museum, London, and known as the Elgin Marbles.
[3] the ocean—as if long unwilling to bear away from Greece the relics of her ancient grandeur.

When the fresh breeze is fair as breeze may be,
The white sails set, the gallant frigate tight,
Masts, spires, and strand retiring to the right,
The glorious main expanding o'er the bow,
The convoy spread like wild swans in their flight,
The dullest sailer wearing[1] bravely now,
So gayly curl the waves before each dashing prow.

XVIII.

And oh, the little warlike world within!
The well-reeved[2] guns, the netted canopy,[3]
The hoarse command, the busy humming din,
When, at a word, the tops are manned on high:
Hark to the Boatswain's call, the cheering cry,
While through the seaman's hand the tackle glides
Or school-boy Midshipman that, standing by,
Strains his shrill pipe, as good or ill betides,
And well the docile crew that skillful urchin guides.

XIX.

White is the glassy deck, without a stain,
Where on the watch the staid Lieutenant walks:
Look on that part which sacred doth remain
For the lone chieftain,[4] who majestic stalks,
Silent and feared by all: not oft he talks
With aught beneath him, if he would preserve
That strict restraint, which broken, ever balks
Conquest and Fame: but Britons rarely swerve
From law, however stern, which tends their strength to nerve.

XX.

Blow! swiftly blow, thou keel-compelling gale!
Till the broad sun withdraws his lessening ray;

---

[1] enduring.   [2] fastened.
[3] net covering to prevent blocks or splinters from falling on deck.   [4] the captain.

Then must the pennant-bearer slacken sail,
That lagging barks may make their lazy way.
Ah! grievance sore, and listless dull delay,
To waste on sluggish hulks the sweetest breeze!
What leagues are lost before the dawn of day,
Thus loitering pensive on the willing seas,
The flapping sails hauled down to halt for logs like these!

XXI.

The moon is up; by Heaven, a lovely eve!
Long streams of light o'er dancing waves expand!
Now lads on shore may sigh, and maids believe:
Such be our fate when we return to land!
Meantime some rude Arion's[1] restless hand
Wakes the brisk harmony that sailors love:
A circle there of merry listeners stand,
Or to some well-known measure[2] featly move,
Thoughtless, as if on shore they still were free to rove.

XXII.

Through Calpe's[3] straits survey the steepy shore;
Europe and Afric, on each other gaze!
Lands of the dark-eyed Maid and dusky Moor,[4]
Alike beheld beneath pale Hecate's blaze:[5]
How softly on the Spanish shore she[6] plays,
Disclosing rock, and slope, and forest brown,
Distinct, though darkening with her waning phase;
But Mauritania's[7] giant shadows frown,
From mountain-cliff to coast descending somber down.

XXIII.

'Tis night, when Meditation bids us feel
We once have loved, though love is at an end:

---

[1] Arion, a famous musician of ancient Greece.   [2] tune.
[3] Calpe, ancient name of Gibraltar.
[4] Spain on one side of the strait and Morocco on the other.
[5] the light of the moon. Hecate was one of the moon-goddesses of the ancients.
[6] the moon.   [7] Mauritania, Roman name of Morocco.

The heart, lone mourner of its baffled zeal,
Though friendless now, will dream it had a friend,
Who with the weight of years would wish to bend,
When Youth itself survives young Love and Joy?
Alas! when mingling souls forget to blend,
Death hath but little left him to destroy!
Ah, happy years! once more who would not be a boy?

. . . . . .

XXV.

To sit on rocks, to muse o'er flood and fell,[1]
To slowly trace the forest's shady scene,
Where things that own not man's dominion dwell,
And mortal foot hath ne'er or rarely been ;
To climb the trackless mountain all unseen,
With the wild flock that never needs a fold ;
Alone o'er steeps and foaming falls to lean :
This is not solitude ; 'tis but to hold
Converse with Nature's charms, and view her stores unrolled.

XXVI.

But midst the crowd, the hum, the shock of men,
To hear, to see, to feel, and to possess,
And roam along, the world's tired denizen,
With none who bless us, none whom we can bless ;
Minions of splendor shrinking from distress !
None that, with kindred consciousness endued,
If we were not, would seem to smile the less
Of all that flattered, followed, sought, and sued :
This is to be alone ; this, this is solitude !

. . . . . .

XXXVII.

Dear Nature is the kindest mother still ;
Though always changing, in her aspect mild :

[1] a stony hill.

From her bare bosom let me take my fill,
Her never-weaned, though not her favored child.
Oh! she is fairest in her features wild,
Where nothing polished dares pollute her path :
To me by day or night she ever smiled,
Though I have marked her when none other hath,
And sought her more and more, and loved her best in
wrath.

XXXVIII.

Land of Albania !¹ where Iskander² rose ;
Theme of the young, and beacon of the wise,
And he his namesake,³ whose oft-baffled foes,
Shrunk from his deeds of chivalrous emprise :⁴
Land of Albania! let me bend mine eyes
On thee, thou rugged nurse of savage men !
The cross descends,⁵ thy minarets⁶ arise,
And the pale crescent⁷ sparkles in the glen,
Through many a cypress grove within each city's ken.

XXXIX.

Childe Harold sailed, and passed the barren spot
Where sad Penelope o'erlooked the wave ;⁸

¹ country north of Greece, bordering the Adriatic Sea.
² Alexander (Turkish form, Iskander) the Great, famous conqueror, who lived three centuries before Christ. He was king of Macedonia, part of which was in Albania.
³ Scanderbeg, or Iskander; called also Lord or Prince Alexander, a famous patriot chief of Albania in the 15th century.
⁴ enterprise.
⁵ referring to the suppression of Christianity in Albania, by the Turks, after the death of Scanderbeg.
⁶ turrets on Mohammedan mosques. " Minarets arise "—meaning the establishment of the Mohammedan (Turkish) religion.
⁷ quarter-moon: the emblem on the Turkish national flag.
⁸ Thiaki, one of the Ionian Islands, west of Greece, anciently called Ithaca, of which the famous Ulysses was king. During his absence at the siege of Troy, and his subsequent wanderings, his wife Penelope watched and waited for him with affectionate devotion.

And onward viewed the mount, not yet forgot,
The lover's refuge, and the Lesbian's grave.[1]
Dark Sappho! could not verse immortal save
That breast imbued with such immortal fire?
Could she not live who life eternal gave?
If life eternal may await the lyre,
That only Heaven to which Earth's children may aspire.

XL.

'Twas on a Grecian autumn's gentle eve,
Childe Harold hailed Leucadia's Cape afar;
A spot he longed to see, nor cared to leave:
Oft did he mark the scenes of vanished war,
Actium,[2] Lepanto,[3] fatal Trafalgar:[4]
Mark them unmoved, for he would not delight
(Born beneath some remote inglorious star)
In themes of bloody fray, or gallant fight,
But loathed the bravo's trade, and laughed at martial wight.[5]

. . . . . .

XLII

Morn dawns; and with it stern Albania's hills,
Dark Suli's rocks,[6] and Pindus'[7] inland peak,

---

[1] a rock on Santa Maura (anciently called Leucadia), one of the Ionian Islands. From this rock, it is said, the Greek poetess Sappho (born in the Island of Lesbos, on the coast of Asia Minor) cast herself into the sea, in a fit of grief and despair at the neglect of a man she loved.

[2] a town and cape (now called Azio) on the west coast of Greece, near which a sea-battle took place in 31 B.C., between the fleets of Octavius (afterwards the Emperor Augustus) and Mark Antony, two opposing leaders in the Roman civil war that followed the death of Julius Cæsar.

[3] a town on the coast of the Gulf of Corinth, Greece, near which the fleets of Spain and several Italian states defeated the Turks in a great battle on October 7, 1571.

[4] a cape on the south coast of Spain, off which, on October 21, 1805, the British Admiral Nelson gained a great victory over the French and Spanish fleets. Nelson himself was killed in this battle.

[5] person.

[6] mountains in Albania.

[7] a mountain chain between Epirus and Thessaly, north of Greece.

Robed half in mist, bedewed with snowy rills,
Arrayed in many a dun and purple streak,
Arise : and as the clouds along them break,
Disclose the dwelling of the mountaineer :
Here roams the wolf, the eagle whets his beak,
Birds, beasts of prey, and wilder men appear,
And gathering storms around convulse the closing year.

XLIII.

Now Harold felt himself at length alone,
And bade to Christian tongues¹ a long adieu :
Now he adventured on a shore unknown,
Which all admire, but many dread to view :
His breast was armed 'gainst fate, his wants were few :
Peril he sought not, but ne'er shrank to meet :
The scene was savage, but the scene was new ;
This made the ceaseless toil of travel sweet ;
Beat back keen winter's blast, and welcomed summer's heat.

. . . .

XLVI.

From the dark barriers of that rugged clime,
E'en to the center of Illyria's² vales,
Childe Harold passed o'er many a mount sublime,
Through lands scarce noticed in historic tales :
Yet in famed Attica³ such lovely dales
Are rarely seen ; nor can fair Tempe⁴ boast
A charm they know not ; loved Parnassus⁵ fails,
Though classic ground,⁶ and consecrated most,
To match some spots that lurk within this lowering coast.

---

¹ Christian languages : meaning Christian people, as he was about to travel in countries inhabited by Mohammedans.
² Illyria, country north of Albania, bordering the Adriatic Sea.
³ ancient name of the district of Greece in which Athens is situated.
⁴ a beautiful valley of Thessaly, a district of ancient Greece.
⁵ see note 5, page 45.
⁶ ground on which occurred great events described in the ancient classics, *i. e.*, celebrated Greek and Latin authors.

XLVII.

He passed bleak Pindus, Acherusia's lake,[1]
And left the primal city [2] of the land,
And onwards did his further journey take
To greet Albania's chief,[3] whose dread command
Is lawless law ; for with a bloody hand
He sways a nation, turbulent and bold ;
Yet here and there some daring mountain-band
Disdain his power, and from their rocky hold
Hurl their defiance far, nor yield, unless to gold.[4]

. . . . . .

LII.

No city's towers pollute the lovely view ;
Unseen is Yanina, though not remote,
Veiled by the screen of hills : here men are few,
Scanty the hamlet, rare the lonely cot ;
But, peering down each precipice, the goat
Browseth : and, pensive o'er his scattered flock,
The little shepherd in his white capote [5]
Doth lean his boyish form along the rock,
Or in his cave awaits the tempest's short-lived shock.

LIII.

Oh ! where, Dodona,[6] is thine aged grove,
Prophetic fount, and oracle divine ?
What valley echoed the response of Jove ? [7]
What trace remaineth of the Thunderer's [8] shrine ?

---

[1] a lake of Epirus, northwest of Greece.
[2] Yanina, chief city of Albania.
[3] the celebrated Ali Pacha, governor of the country.
[4] the Castle of Suli was held for eighteen years against 30,000 Albanians, but was at last taken by bribery.
[5] cape ; cloak.
[6] an ancient city of Epirus where there were a famous temple of Jupiter, and an oak tree, from the boughs of which the god delivered oracles, or prophecies, to those who came to consult him.
[7] another name of Jupiter.
[8] as god of the heavens, Jupiter was called the Thunderer.

All, all forgotten—and shall man repine
That his frail bonds to fleeting life are broke ?
Cease, fool ! the fate of gods may well be thine :
Wouldst thou survive the marble or the oak,
When nations, tongues, and words must sink beneath
    the stroke ?

LIV.

Epirus' bounds recede, and mountains fail ;
Tired of upgazing still, the wearied eye
Reposes gladly on as smooth a vale
As ever Spring yclad in grassy dye :
Ev'n on a plain no humble beauties lie,
Where some bold river breaks the long expanse,
And woods along the banks are waving high,
Whose shadows in the glassy waters dance,
Or with the moonbeam sleep in Midnight's solemn trance.

LV.

The sun had sunk behind vast Tomerit,[1]
The Laos'[2] wide and fierce came roaring by ;
The shades of wonted night were gathering yet,
When, down the steep banks winding wearily
Childe Harold saw, like meteors in the sky,
The glittering minarets of Tepalen,[3]
Whose walls o'erlook the stream ; and drawing nigh,
He heard the busy hum of warrior-men
Swelling the breeze that sighed along the lengthening
    glen.

LVI.

He passed the sacred Haram's[4] silent tower,
And underneath the wide o'erarching gate

[1] a mountain of Epirus; anciently called Tomarus.
[2] a river of Albania.
[3] the country palace of Ali Pacha.
[4] haram, apartments occupied by the females in dwelling-houses in Turkey and other countries of the East.

Surveyed the dwelling of this chief of power,[1]
Where all around proclaimed his high estate.
Amidst no common pomp the despot sate,
While busy preparation shook the court ;
Slaves, eunuchs,[2] soldiers, guests, and santons[3] wait
Within, a palace, and without, a fort,
Here men of every clime appear to make resort.

LVII.

Richly caparisoned, a ready row
Of armèd horse, and many a warlike store,
Circled the wide-extending court below ;
Above, strange groups adorned the corridor ;
And oft-times through the area's echoing door,
Some high-capped Tartar[4] spurred his steed away ;
The Turk, the Greek, the Albanian and the Moor,
Here mingled in their many-hued array,
While the deep war-drum's sound announced the close of
  day.

LVIII.

The wild Albanian kirtled[5] to his knee,
With shawl-girt head and ornamented gun,
And gold-embroidered garments, fair to see :
The crimson-scarfèd men of Macedon ;[6]
The Delhi[7] with his cap of terror on,
And crooked glaive ; the lively, supple Greek ;

. . . . . .

The bearded Turk, that rarely deigns to speak,
Master of all around, too potent to be meek,

---

[1] Ali Pacha. [2] guards or attendants of the Haram.
[3] religious Turks, regarded by the people as saints.
[4] native of Tartary, a country of Asia ; formerly applied also to a native of southwestern Russia, bordering Turkey. [5] kirtle, a gown ; a mantle.
[6] Macedonia, country east of Albania. [7] horseman.

CHILDE HAROLD. 77

LIX.

Are mixed conspicuous ;[1] some recline in groups,
Scanning the motley scene that varies round ;
There some grave Moslem[2] to devotion stoops,
And some that smoke, and some that play are found ;
Here the Albanian proudly treads the ground :
Half-whispering there the Greek is heard to prate :
Hark ! from the mosque the nightly solemn sound,
The muezzin's[3] call doth shake the minaret,
"There is no god but God!—to prayer—lo! God is great ! "

LX.

Just at this season Ramazani's fast[4]
Through the long day its penance did maintain.
But when the lingering twilight hour was past,
Revel and feast assumed the rule again :
Now all was bustle, and the menial train
Prepared and spread the plenteous board within ;
The vacant gallery now seemed made in vain,
But from the chambers came the mingling din,
As page and slave anon[5] were passing out and in.

---

[1] Byron, in a letter to his mother, after his visit to Ali Pacha, thus describes the scene at the palace :
" The Albanians in their dresses (the most magnificent in the world, consisting of a long white kilt, gold-worked cloak, crimson velvet gold-laced jacket and waistcoat, silver-mounted pistols and daggers) ; the Tartars with their high caps ; the Turks in their vast pelisses and turbans ; the soldiers and black slaves with the horses, the former in groups, in an immense large open gallery in front of the palace, the latter placed in a kind of cloister below it ; two hundred steeds ready caparisoned to move in a moment ; couriers entering or passing out with despatches ; the kettle-drums beating ; boys calling the hour from the minaret of the mosque ;—altogether, with the singular appearance of the building itself, formed a new and delightful spectacle to a stranger."
[2] Mussulman ; Mohammedan.
[3] The muezzin, or chanter, calls the people to prayer from the minaret of the mosque. He cries out in a loud voice such words as, "There is no god but God ; Mohammed is God's prophet ; come to prayer ; God is great." The Mohammedans pray five times a day.
[4] Ramazan, or Ramadan, the ninth month of the Mohammedan year, is the Turkish Lent, or fasting season. In this month strict fast is kept during the daytime, but at night feasting and amusements are carried on.
[5] frequently.

LXII.

In marble-paved pavilion, where a spring
Of living water from the center rose,
Whose bubbling did a genial freshness fling,
And soft voluptuous couches breathed repose,
Ali reclined, a man of war and woes :
Yet in his lineaments ye can not trace,
While Gentleness her milder radiance throws
Along that aged venerable face,
The deeds that lurk beneath, and stain him with disgrace.[1]

. . . . . .

LXIV.

Mid many things most new to ear and eye,
The pilgrim rested here his weary feet,
And gazed around on Moslem luxury,
Till quickly wearied with that spacious seat
Of Wealth and Wantonness,[1] the choice retreat
Of sated Grandeur from the city's noise.
And were it humbler, it in sooth were sweet :
But Peace abhorreth artificial joys,
And Pleasure, leagued with Pomp, the zest of both destroys.

LXV.

Fierce are Albani's children, yet they lack
Not virtues, were those virtues more mature.
Where is the foe that ever saw their back ?[2]
Who can so well the toil of war endure ?
Their native fastnesses not more secure
Than they in doubtful time of troublous need :
Their wrath how deadly ! but their friendship sure,
When Gratitude or Valor bids them bleed,
Unshaken rushing on where'er their chief may lead.

---

[1] Ali Pacha was a ferocious and cruel man, though he did much good in Albania by suppressing bands of robbers, constructing roads, and maintaining order and justice.

[2] meaning that they never ran away in a fight, through fear of the foe.

LXVI.

Childe Harold saw them in their chieftain's tower,
Thronging to war in splendor and success ;
And after viewed them, when, within their power,
Himself awhile the victim of distress :
That saddening hour when bad men hotlier press :
But these did shelter him beneath their roof,
When less barbarians would have cheered him less.
And fellow-countrymen have stood aloof—
In aught that tries the heart how few withstand the proof!

LXVII.

It chanced that adverse winds once drove his bark
Full on the coast of Suli's shaggy shore,[1]
When all around was desolate and dark ;
To land was perilous, to sojourn more ;
Yet for a while the mariners forebore,
Dubious to trust where treachery might lurk :
At length they ventured forth, though doubting sore
That those who loathe alike the Frank [2] and Turk
Might once again renew their ancient butcher-work.

LXVIII.

Vain fear ! the Suliotes stretched the welcome hand,
Led them o'er rocks and past the dangerous swamp,
Kinder than polished slaves, though not so bland,
And piled the hearth, and wrung their garments damp,
And filled the bowl, and trimmed the cheerful lamp,
And spread the fare : though homely, all they had :
Such conduct bears Philanthropy's rare stamp—
To rest the weary and to soothe the sad,
Doth lesson [3] happier men, and shame at least the bad.

[1] the coast of Epirus.

[2] the French. Ali Pacha, in his war against the Suliotes was aided by the French ; hence the Suliotes hated the Frank as well as the Turk.

[3] here a verb, meaning to teach.

LXIX.

It came to pass, that when he did address
Himself to quit at length this mountain land,
Combined marauders half-way barred egress,
And wasted far and near with glaive and brand ;
And therefore did he take a trusty band
To traverse Acarnania's [1] forest wide,
In war well seasoned, and with labors tanned,
Till he did greet white Achelous'[2] tide,
And from his further bank Ætolia's [3] wolds espied.

LXX.

Where lone Utraikey [4] forms its circling cove,
And weary waves retire to gleam at rest,
How brown the foliage of the green hill's grove,
Nodding at midnight o'er the calm bay's breast,
As winds come whispering lightly from the west,
Kissing, not ruffling, the blue deep's serene :
Here Harold was received a welcome guest ;
Nor did he pass unmoved the gentle scene,
For many a joy could he from night's soft presence glean.

LXXI.

On the smooth shore the night-fires brightly blazed,
The feast was done, the red wine circling fast,
And he that unawares had there ygazed
With gaping wonderment had stared aghast ;
For ere night's midmost, stillest hour was past,
The native revels of the troop began ;
Each palikar [5] his saber from him cast,

---

[1] Acarnania, a mountainous district in the northwest of Greece, bordering the Ionian Sea.
[2] a river of Acarnania, now called Aspropotamo, *i. e.*, White River, from the cream color of its waters.
[3] Ætolia, a district of North Greece, lying east of Acarnania.
[4] a small place situated in one of the bays of the Gulf of Arta, on the northwest coast of Greece, between Epirus and Acarnania.
[5] soldier ; properly, a lad.

And bounding hand in hand, man linked to man,
Yelling their uncouth dirge, long danced the kirtled clan.

LXXII.

Childe Harold at a little distance stood,
And viewed, but not displeased, the revelrie,
Nor hated harmless mirth, however rude:
In sooth, it was no vulgar sight to see
Their barbarous, yet their not indecent glee:
And as the flames along their faces gleamed,
Their gestures nimble, dark eyes flashing free,
The long wild locks that to their girdles streamed,
While thus in concert they this lay half sung, half
   screamed:

Tambourgi![1] Tambourgi! thy 'larum afar
Gives hope to the valiant, and promise of war;
All the sons of the mountains arise at the note,
Chimariot, Illyrian, and dark Suliote![2]

Oh! who is more brave than a dark Suliote,
In his snowy camese[3] and his shaggy capote?
To the wolf and the vulture he leaves his wild flock,
And descends to the plain like the stream from the rock.

Shall the sons of Chimari, who never forgive
The fault of a friend, bid an enemy live?
Let those guns so unerring such vengeance forego?
What mark is so fair as the breast of a foe?

Macedonia sends forth her invincible race;
For a time they abandon the cave and the chase:
But those scarves of blood-red shall be redder, before
The saber is sheathed and the battle is o'er.

[1] drummer; one who beats the drum.
[2] belonging to Chimari, Illyria, and Suli, districts of Albania.
[3] garment covering the body.

Then the pirates of Parga[1] that dwell by the waves,
And teach the pale Franks what it is to be slaves,
Shall leave on the beach the long galley and oar,
And track to his covert the captive on shore.

I ask not the pleasure that riches supply,
My saber shall win what the feeble must buy :
Shall win the young bride with her long flowing hair,
And many a maid from her mother shall tear.

I love the fair face of the maid in her youth ;
Her caresses shall lull me, her music shall soothe :
Let her bring from her chamber the many-toned lyre,
And sing us a song on the fall of her sire.

Remember the moment when Previsa[2] fell,
The shrieks of the conquered, the conqueror's yell ;
The roofs that we fired, and the plunder we shared,
The wealthy we slaughter'd, the lovely we spared.

I talk not of mercy, I talk not of fear ;
He neither must know who would serve the Vizier ;[3]
Since the days of our prophet the crescent ne'er saw
A chief ever glorious like Ali Pashaw.[4]

. . . . . .

Selictar ![5] unsheath then our chief's scimitar :
Tambourgi ! thy 'larum gives promise of war.
Ye mountains that see us descend to the shore,
Shall view us as victors, or view us no more !

LXXIII.

Fair Greece ! sad relic of departed worth !
Immortal, though no more ;[6] though fallen, great !

---

[1] a sea-coast town of Epirus.
[2] a sea-coast town of Epirus, taken by the Albanians from the French.
[3] meaning Ali Pacha. Vizier, chief minister of a Turkish or other Eastern sovereign. Ali Pacha was so called, being ruler of Albania under the authority of the Sultan (king) of Turkey.   [4] spelled Pacha, Pasha, or Pashaw ; means governor or viceroy.
[5] sword-bearer.   [6] though its ancient glory has departed.

Who now shall lead thy scattered children forth,
And long accustomed bondage uncreate ?
Not such thy sons who whilome did await,
The hopeless warriors of a willing doom,
In bleak Thermopylæ's [1] sepulchral strait—
Oh, who that gallant spirit shall resume,
Leap from Eurotas' [2] banks, and call thee from the tomb?

. . . . .

LXXV.

In all save form alone, how changed ! [3] and who
That marks the fire still sparkling in each eye,
Who but would deem their bosoms burned anew
With thy unquenchèd beam. lost Liberty ! [4]
And many dream withal the hour is nigh
That gives them back their fathers' heritage :
For foreign arms and aid they fondly sigh,
Nor solely dare encounter hostile rage,
Or tear their name defiled from Slavery's mournful page.

LXXVI.

Hereditary bondsmen ! know ye not
Who would be free themselves must strike the blow ?
By their right arms the conquest must be wrought !
Will Gaul [5] or Muscovite [6] redress ye ? No !
True, they may lay your proud despoilers [7] low,

---

[1] Thermopylæ, a narrow mountain pass between Thessaly and Locris (north Greece). Here, in 480 B.C., took place the famous battle in which Leonidas, King of Sparta (a country of Greece), resisted the advance of the Persian King Xerxes, who had come with a great army to invade the country. Leonidas and his little band, numbering only three hundred, fought until they were all killed but one man, who carried the news to Sparta.
[2] a river of Sparta.
[3] meaning the modern Greeks.
[4] At the time that Byron wrote. Greece was under the oppressive rule of Turkey. She became an independent kingdom in 1829.
[5] Frenchman.
[6] Russian. Muscovy was formerly the name of Russia.
[7] the Turks.

But not for you will Freedom's altars flame.
Shades of the Helots!¹ triumph o'er your foe :
Greece! change thy lords, thy state is still the same :
Thy glorious day is o'er, but not thy years of shame.

. . . . .

LXXXIII.

This must he feel, the true-born son of Greece,
If Greece one true-born patriot still can boast :
Not such as prate of war, but skulk in peace,
The bondsman's peace, who sighs for all he lost,
Yet with smooth smile his tyrant can accost,
And wield the slavish sickle, not the sword :
Ah, Greece! they love thee least who owe thee most—
Their birth, their blood, and that sublime record
Of hero sires, who shame thy now degenerate horde!²

. . . . .

LXXXV.

And yet how lovely in thine age of woe,
Land of lost gods and godlike men, art thou !
Thy vales of evergreen, thy hills of snow,³
Proclaim thee Nature's varied favorite now ;
Thy fanes, thy temples, to thy surface bow,
Commingling slowly with heroic earth,
Broke by the share of every rustic plough ;
So perish monuments of mortal birth,
So perish all in turn, save well-recorded Worth ;

LXXXVI.

Save where some solitary column mourns
Above its prostrate brethren of the cave ;⁴

---

¹ the population of ancient Sparta was divided into four classes, one of which was formed of serfs or slaves, who were called Helots.

² referring to the native people of Greece, who, by submitting to Turkish rule, dishonored the memory of their great ancestors.

³ on some of the mountains of Greece the snow is never entirely melted.

⁴ the cave or quarries of Mount Pentelicus, in Attica, where the marble was obtained for the magnificent temples and monuments of Athens.

Save where Tritonia's¹ airy shrine adorns
Colonna's cliff,² and gleams along the wave;
Save o'er some warrior's half-forgotten grave,
Where the gray stones and unmolested grass
Ages, but not oblivion, feebly brave,
While strangers only not regardless pass,
Lingering like me, perchance, to gaze, and sigh " Alas!"

LXXXVII.

Yet are thy skies as blue, thy crags as wild;
Sweet are thy groves, and verdant are thy fields,
Thine olives ripe as when Minerva smiled,
And still his honey'd wealth Hymettus³ yields;
There the blithe bee his fragrant fortress builds,
The free-born wanderer of thy mountain air;
Apollo still thy long, long summer gilds,
Still in his beam Mendeli's⁴ marbles glare;
Art, Glory, Freedom fail, but Nature still is fair.

LXXXVIII.

Where'er we tread 'tis haunted, holy ground;
No earth of thine is lost in vulgar mold,
But one vast realm of wonder spreads around,
And all the Muse's tales seem truly told,
Till the sense aches with gazing to behold
The scenes our earliest dreams have dwelt upon:
Each hill and dale, each deepening glen and wold,
Defies the power which crush'd thy temples gone:
Age shakes Athena's tower, but spares gray Marathon.⁵

· · · · · · · ·

¹ Tritonia was another name of Pallas Minerva, the goddess of wisdom.

² Cape Colonna, in the south of Attica, where there was a temple of Pallas, which could be seen from a great distance at sea.

³ a mountain of Attica, celebrated for the excellent honey found there.

⁴ Mendeli, the modern name of Mount Pentelicus. (See note 4, page 84.)

⁵ a plain on the east coast of Attica, twenty miles from Athens, famous as the place where, in 490 B.C., an Athenian army of 10,000 men, under Miltiades, defeated a Persian army of over 100,000 under Datis and Artaphernes, the generals of Darius, King of Persia.

XC.

. . . . . .
What sacred trophy marks the hallow'd ground,
Recording Freedom's smile and Asia's tear?
The rifled urn, the violated mound,[1]
The dust thy courser's hoof, rude stranger! spurns around.

XCI.

Yet to the remnants of thy splendor past
Shall pilgrims, pensive, but unwearied, throng:
Long shall the voyager, with th' Ionian blast,
Hail the bright clime of battle and of song;
Long shall thine annals and immortal tongue
Fill with thy fame the youth of many a shore:
Boast of the aged! lesson of the young!
Which sages venerate and bards adore,
As Pallas and the Muse unveil their awful lore.

XCII.

The parted bosom clings to wonted home,
If aught that's kindred cheer the welcome hearth;
He that is lonely, hither[2] let him roam,
And gaze complacent on congenial earth.
Greece is no lightsome land of social mirth;
But he whom Sadness sootheth may abide,
And scarce regret the region of his birth,
When wandering slow by Delphi's sacred side,
Or gazing o'er the plains where Greek and Persian died.

XCIII.

Let such approach this consecrated land,
And pass in peace along the magic waste;
But spare its relics—let no busy hand
Deface the scenes, already how defaced!
Not for such purpose were these altars placed.

---

[1] on the field of Marathon, covering the graves of the Greeks who fell in the battle.
[2] to Greece.

Revere the remnants nations once revered ;
So may our country's name [1] be undisgraced,
So mayst thou prosper where thy youth was rear'd,
By every honest joy of love and life endear'd !

. . . . . .

CANTO THE THIRD.

I.

Is thy face like thy mother's, my fair child !
Ada ! sole daughter of my house and heart ? [2]
When last I saw thy young blue eyes they smiled,
And then we parted,—not as now we part,
But with a hope.—
         Awaking with a start,
The waters heave around me ; and on high
The winds lift up their voices : I depart,
Whither I know not ; but the hour's gone by,
When Albion's lessening shores could grieve or glad
    mine eyes.

II.

Once more upon the waters ! yet once more !
And the waves bound beneath me as a steed
That knows his rider. Welcome to their roar !
Swift be their guidance, wheresoe'er it lead !
Though the strain'd mast should quiver as a reed,
And the rent canvas fluttering strew the gale,
Still must I on ; for I am as a weed,
Flung from the rock, on Ocean's foam, to sail
Where'er the surge may sweep, the tempest's breath
    prevail.

. . . . . .

[1] England's.   [2] Byron's own daughter and only child, Ada.

IV.

Since my young days of passion—joy, or pain,
Perchance my heart and harp have lost a string,
And both may jar : it may be, that in vain
I would essay as I have sung to sing.
Yet, though a dreary strain, to this I cling,
So that it wean me from the weary dream
Of selfish grief or gladness—so it fling
Forgetfulness around me—it shall seem
To me, though to none else, a not ungrateful theme.

. . . . . .

VIII.

. . . . . .

Long-absent Harold reappears at last ;
He of the breast which fain no more would feel,
Wrung with the wounds which kill not, but ne'er heal ;
Yet Time, who changes all, had alter'd him
In soul and aspect as in age : years steal
Fire from the mind as vigor from the limb ;
And life's enchanted cup but sparkles near the brim.

. . . . . .

X.

Secure in guarded coldness, he had mix'd
Again in fancied safety with his kind,
And deemed his spirit now so firmly fix'd
And sheathed with an invulnerable mind,
That, if no joy, no sorrow lurk'd behind ;
And he, as one, might 'midst the many stand
Unheeded, searching through the crowd to find
Fit speculation ; such as in strange land
He found in wonder-works of God and Nature's hand.

. . . . . .

XIII.

Where rose the mountains, there to him were friends ;
Where roll'd the ocean, thereon was his home ;

Where a blue sky, and glowing clime, extends,
He had the passion and the power to roam ;
The desert, forest, cavern, breaker's foam,
Were unto him companionship : they spake
A mutual language, clearer than the tome
Of his land's tongue,[1] which he would oft forsake
For nature's pages glass'd by sunbeams on the lake.

. . . . . .

XVI.

Self-exiled Harold wanders forth again,
With naught of hope left, but with less of gloom,
The very knowledge that he lived in vain,
That all was over on this side the tomb.
Had made Despair a smilingness assume,
Which, though 'twere wild,—as on the plunder'd wreck
When mariners would madly meet their doom
With draughts intemperate on the sinking deck—
Did yet inspire a cheer, which he forbore to check.

XVII.

Stop !—for thy tread is on an Empire's dust ![2]
An Earthquake's spoil is sepulchred below !
Is the spot mark'd with no colossal bust ?
Nor column trophied for triumphal show ?
None ; but the moral's truth tells simpler so,
As the ground was before, thus let it be :—
How that red rain[3] hath made the harvest grow !
And is this all the world has gain'd by thee,
Thou first and last of fields ! king-making Victory ?

[1] the English language.
[2] the field of Waterloo in Belgium, where, on June 18. 1815, was fought the great battle in which the French, under Napoleon Bonaparte, were defeated by the British and Prussians under Wellington and Blücher. By this defeat Napoleon lost the French Empire he had established, and soon afterwards he was sent a prisoner to the island of St. Helena, where he died in 1821.
[3] of blood shed in the battle.

XVIII.

And Harold stands upon this place of skulls,
The grave of France, the deadly Waterloo!
How in an hour the power which gave annuls
Its gifts, transferring fame as fleeting too!
In "pride of place"¹ here last the eagle² flew,
Then tore with bloody talon the rent plain,
Pierced by the shaft of banded nations through;
Ambition's life and labors all were vain;
He wears the shatter'd links of the world's broken chain.³

. . . . . .

XXI.

There was a sound of revelry by night,⁴
And Belgium's capital had gather'd then
Her Beauty and her Chivalry,⁵ and bright
The lamps shone o'er fair women and brave men;
A thousand hearts beat happily; and when
Music arose with its voluptuous swell,
Soft eyes look'd love to eyes which spake again,
And all went merry as a marriage-bell:
But hush! hark! a deep sound strikes like a rising knell!

XXII.

Did ye not hear it? No; 'twas but the wind
Or the car rattling o'er the stony street;
On with the dance! let joy be unconfined;
No sleep till morn, when Youth and Pleasure meet
To chase the glowing Hours with flying feet—

---

[1] In the old-time sport of falconry—hunting wild fowl by means of hawks—the phrase, "pride of place" meant the highest pitch or point of flight.

[2] Napoleon.

[3] the chain with which Napoleon by his numerous conquests had bound nearly the whole of Europe, was broken by his defeat at Waterloo, and he himself wore the "shattered links" in his imprisonment at St. Helena.

[4] On the night before the battle of Waterloo, Wellington, the British general, and his officers were present at a ball in Brussels, the capital of Belgium. The battle-field is within twelve miles of that city.

[5] gallant men and fair ladies.

But hark!—that heavy sound breaks in once more,
As if the clouds its echo would repeat ;
And nearer, clearer, deadlier than before !
Arm ! arm ! it is—it is—the cannon's opening roar !

XXIII.

Within a windowed niche of that high hall [1]
Sate Brunswick's fated chieftain ; [2] he did hear
That sound the first amidst the festival,
And caught its tone with Death's prophetic ear ;
And when they smiled because he deemed it near,
His heart more truly knew that peal too well
Which stretched his father on a bloody bier, [3]
And roused the vengeance blood alone could quell :
He rushed into the field, and, foremost fighting, fell.

XXIV.

Ah ! then and there was hurrying to and fro,
And gathering tears, and tremblings of distress,
And cheeks all pale, which but an hour ago
Blushed at the praise of their own loveliness ;
And there were sudden partings, such as press
The life from out young hearts, and choking sighs
Which ne'er might be repeated : who would guess
If ever more should meet those mutual eyes,
Since upon night so sweet such awful morn could rise !

XXV.

And there was mounting in hot haste : the steed,
The mustering squadron, and the clattering car,
Went pouring forward with impetuous speed,

---

[1] in which the ball was given.
[2] the Duke of Brunswick.
[3] the Duke of Brunswick's father was fatally wounded at the battle of Jena (Germany), October 14, 1806, in which the Prussians under the Prince of Hohenlohe were defeated by the French under Napoleon.

And swiftly forming in the ranks of war;
And the deep thunder peal on peal afar;
And near, the beat of the alarming drum
Roused up the soldier ere the morning star;
While thronged the citizens with terror dumb,
Or whispering, with white lips—"The foe! they come!
  they come!"

XXVI.

And wild and high the "Cameron's gathering"[1] rose,
The war-note of Lochiel,[2] which Albyn's[3] hills
Have heard, and heard, too, have her Saxon foes:[4]
How in the noon of night that pibroch[5] thrills
Savage and shrill! But with the breath which fills
Their mountain-pipe, so fill the mountaineers
With the fierce native daring which instills
The stirring memory of a thousand years,
And Evan's, Donald's[6] fame rings in each clansman's[7]
  ears.

XXVII.

And Ardennes[8] waves above them her green leaves,
Dewy with Nature's tear-drops, as they pass,
Grieving, if aught inanimate e'er grieves,
Over the unreturning brave,—alas!
Ere evening to be trodden like the grass

---

[1] one of the tunes of the Cameron Highlanders, the name given to the 79th regiment of infantry in the British army, so called from the name of the officer who raised the corps.

[2] The Camerons of Lochiel (Scotland) were famed in Scottish history for their valor and achievements in war.

[3] Albyn, ancient name of the Scottish Highlands (north part of Scotland).

[4] in the wars of former times between the Scotch and the English (Saxons).

[5] a sort of wild music performed on the Scottish bagpipe.

[6] Sir Evan Cameron and his descendant Donald were distinguished chiefs of the Camerons of Lochiel.

[7] The clans of the Scottish Highlands in former times were tribes or families of the same name united under a chieftain, by whom they were led in war. Each clan was designated by the common name, as the clan Cameron, the clan Stuart.

[8] a range of hills, many of them covered with forests of oak and beech, extending through parts of Belgium and northeast France.

Which now beneath them, but above shall grow
In its next verdure, when this fiery mass
Of living valor, rolling on the foe,
And burning with high hope, shall molder cold and low.

XXVIII.

Last noon beheld them full of lusty life,
Last eve in Beauty's circle proudly gay,
The midnight brought the signal-sound of strife,
The morn the marshaling in arms,—the day
Battle's magnificently stern array!
The thunder-clouds close o'er it, which when rent
The earth is covered thick with other clay,
Which her own clay shall cover, heaped and pent,
Rider and horse,—friend, foe,—in one red burial blent![1]

. . . .

XXXVI.

There sunk the greatest, nor the worst of men,[2]
Whose spirit antithetically[3] mixt,
One moment of the mightiest, and again
On little objects with like firmness fixt;
Extreme in all things! hadst thou[2] been betwixt,
Thy throne had still been thine, or never been:
For daring made thy rise as fall: thou seek'st
Even now to reassume the imperial mien,
And shake again the world, the Thunderer of the scene!

XXXVII.

Conqueror and captive of the earth art thou![4]
She trembles at thee still, and thy wild name

---

[1] The foregoing stanzas, describing the eve and morning of Waterloo, are much admired by readers of Byron. One of the ablest of British critics has observed that "there can be no more remarkable proof of the greatness of Lord Byron's genius than the spirit and interest he has contrived to communicate to his picture of the oft-drawn and difficult scene of the breaking up from Brussels before the great battle."
[2] Napoleon.   [3] in contrast or opposition.
[4] Napoleon is still referred to in this and the following stanza.

Was ne'er more bruited in men's minds than now
That thou art nothing, save the jest of Fame,
Who wooed thee once, thy vassal, and became
The flatterer of thy fierceness, till thou wert
A god unto thyself; nor less the same
To the astounded kingdoms all inert,
Who deemed thee for a time whate'er thou didst assert.

XXXVIII.

Oh, more or less than man—in high or low,
Battling with nations, flying from the field;
Now making monarchs' necks thy footstool, now
More than thy meanest soldier taught to yield:
An empire thou couldst crush, command, rebuild,
But govern not thy pettiest passion, nor,
However deeply in men's spirits skilled,
Look through thine own, nor curb the lust of war,
Nor learn that tempted Fate will leave the loftiest star.

. . . . . .

XLV.

He who ascends to mountain-tops, shall find
The loftiest peaks most wrapt in clouds and snow;
He who surpasses or subdues mankind,
Must look down on the hate of those below.
Though high *above* the sun of glory glow,
And far *beneath* the earth and ocean spread,
Round him are icy rocks, and loudly blow
Contending tempests on his naked head,
And thus reward the toils which to those summits led.

XLVI.

Away with these; true Wisdom's world will be
Within its own creation, or in thine,
Maternal Nature! for who teems like thee,
Thus on the banks of thy majestic Rhine?[1]

[1] the great river of Germany.

There Harold gazes on a work divine,
A blending of all beauties ; streams and dells,
Fruit, foliage, crag, wood, corn-field, mountain, vine,
And chiefless castles [1] breathing stern farewells
From gray but leafy walls, where Ruin greenly dwells.

. . . . . .

LI.

A thousand battles [2] have assailed thy banks,
But these and half their fame have passed away,
And Slaughter heaped on high its weltering ranks :
Their very graves are gone, and what are they ?
Thy tide washed down the blood of yesterday,
And all was stainless, and on thy clear stream
Glassed with its dancing light the sunny ray ;
But o'er the blackened memory's blighting dream
Thy waves would vainly roll, all sweeping as they seem.

LII.

Thus Harold inly said, and passed along,
Yet not insensibly to all which here
Awoke the jocund birds to early song
In glens which might have made even exile dear :
Though on his brow were graven lines austere,
And tranquil sternness which had ta'en the place
Of feelings fierier far but less severe,
Joy was not always absent from his face,
But o'er it in such scenes would steal with transient
trace.

LIII.

Nor was all love shut from him, though his days
Of passion had consumed themselves to dust.
It is in vain that we would coldly gaze
On such as smile upon us ; the heart must

---

[1] The number of castles and cities along the course of the Rhine on both sides is very great, and their situations are remarkably beautiful. Many of the castles are in ruins.
[2] many great battles have been fought on or near the banks of the Rhine.

Leap kindly back to kindness, though disgust
Hath weaned it from all worldlings; thus he felt,
For there was soft remembrance, and sweet trust
In one fond breast, to which his own would melt,
And in its tenderer hour on that his bosom dwelt.

. . . . . .

LV.

That love was pure, and, far above disguise,
Had stood the test of mortal enmities
Still undivided, and cemented more
By peril, dreaded most in female eyes;
But this was firm, and from a foreign shore
Well to that heart might his these absent greetings pour!

The castled crag of Drachenfels [1]
Frowns o'er the wide and winding Rhine,
Whose breast of waters broadly swells
Between the banks which bear the vine,
And hills all rich with blossom'd trees,
And fields which promise corn and wine,
And scattered cities crowning these,
Whose far white walls along them shine,
Have strew'd a scene, which I should see
With double joy wert *thou* with me!

And peasant girls, with deep blue eyes,
And hands which offer early flowers,
Walk smiling o'er this paradise;
Above, the frequent feudal towers [2]

---

[1] The castle of Drachenfels stands on the highest summit of the "Seven Mountains" over the Rhine banks. It is in ruins, and some strange stories are connected with it.

[2] the towers or castles of the great land-holders under the feudal system of former times. In those times the tenant or occupier of the land was bound to serve his superior lord—a duke or a king—in his wars, hence the word feudal, from feud, which means a quarrel.

Through green leaves lift their walls of gray,
And many a rock which deeply lowers,
And noble arch in proud decay,
Look o'er this vale of vintage-bowers :
But one thing want these banks of Rhine,—
Thy gentle hand to clasp in mine !

I send the lilies given to me :
Though long before thy hand they touch,
I know that they must withered be,
But yet reject them not as such ;
For I have cherish'd them as dear,
Because they yet may meet thine eye,
And guide thy soul to mine even here,
When thou behold'st them drooping nigh,
And know'st them gathered by the Rhine,
And offer'd from my heart to thine !

The river nobly foams and flows,
The charm of this enchanted ground,
And all its thousand turns disclose
Some fresher beauty varying round ;
The haughtiest breast its wish might bound
Through life to dwell delighted here ;
Nor could on earth a spot be found
To Nature and to me so dear,
Could thy dear eyes in following mine
Still sweeten more these banks of Rhine !

LVI.

By Coblentz,[1] on a rise of gentle ground,
There is a small and simple pyramid,
Crowning the summit of the verdant mound ;
Beneath its base are heroes' ashes hid,

[1] a town of Rhenish Prussia, on the left bank of the Rhine.

Our enemy's,¹—but let not that forbid
Honor to Marceau !² o'er whose early tomb
Tears, big tears, gushed from the rough soldier's lid,
Lamenting and yet envying such a doom,
Falling for France, whose rights he battled to resume.

LVII.

Brief, brave, and glorious was his young career,—
His mourners were two hosts, his friends and foes;
And fitly may the stranger lingering here
Pray for his gallant spirit's bright repose;
For he was Freedom's champion, one of those,
The few in number, who had not o'erstept
The charter to chastise which she³ bestows
On such as wield her weapons ; he had kept
The whiteness of his soul, and thus men o'er him wept.

LVIII.

Here Ehrenbreitstein,⁴ with her shattered wall
Black with the miner's blast, upon her height
Yet shows of what she was, when shell and ball
Rebounding idly on her strength did light ;
A tower of victory ! from whence the flight
Of baffled foes was watched along the plain :
But Peace destroyed what War could never blight,⁵
And laid those proud roofs bare to Summer's rain—
On which the iron shower for years had poured in vain.

---

¹ England's.
² a young French general killed at the battle of Altenkirchen (Prussia), September 16, 1796.
³ Freedom.
⁴ a town and fortress of Rhenish Prussia, on the right bank of the Rhine, opposite Coblentz. The fortress, built on the summit of a precipitous rock 490 feet high, is one of the strongest in Europe.
⁵ the French took Ehrenbreitstein in 1799, after a siege of fourteen months. Peace being made in 1801, they left the fort, but before their departure they blew up the works.

LIX.

Adieu to thee, fair Rhine ! How long delighted,
The stranger fain would linger on his way !
Thine is a scene alike where souls united
Or lonely Contemplation thus might stray ;
And could the ceaseless vultures [1] cease to prey
On self-condemning bosoms, it were here,
Where Nature, nor too somber nor too gay,
Wild but not rude, awful yet not austere,
Is to the mellow Earth as Autumn to the year.

. . . . . .

LXII.

But these [2] recede. Above me are the Alps, [3]
The palaces of Nature, whose vast walls
Have pinnacled in clouds their snowy scalps,
And throned Eternity in icy halls [4]
Of cold sublimity, where forms and falls
The avalanche—the thunder-bolt of snow !
All that expands the spirit, yet appalls,
Gather around these summits, as to show
How Earth may pierce to Heaven, yet leave vain man below.

LXIII.

But ere these matchless heights I dare to scan.
There is a spot should not be passed in vain,—
Morat ! [5] the proud, the patriot field ! where man
May gaze on ghastly trophies of the slain.

---

[1] birds which feed on dead bodies. The word is here used figuratively for thoughts which torment the mind.

[2] the beauties of the Rhine.

[3] the highest mountain range of Europe—between Switzerland and Italy, and extending into the adjacent countries.

[4] referring to the perpetual snow and the glaciers on the top of the Alps.

[5] a town of Switzerland, where, in a great battle on June 22, 1476, the Swiss defeated Charles the Bold, Duke of Burgundy (France), who had come with a great army to conquer their country.

Nor blush for those who conquered on that plain;
Here Burgundy bequeathed his tombless host,
A bony heap,¹ through ages to remain,
Themselves their monument;—the Stygian coast²
Unsepulchred they roamed, and shrieked each wandering ghost.

LXIV.

While Waterloo with Cannæ's carnage³ vies,
Morat and Marathon twin names shall stand;
They were true Glory's stainless victories,
Won by the unambitious heart and hand
Of a proud, brotherly, and civic band,
All unbought champions in no princely cause
Or vice-entailed Corruption; they no land
Doomed to bewail the blasphemy of laws
Making kings' rights divine, by some Draconic⁴ clause.

. . . .

LXVIII.

Lake Leman⁵ woos me with its crystal face,
The mirror where the stars and mountains view
The stillness of their aspect in each trace
Its clear depth yields of their far height and hue:
There is too much of man here, to look through
With a fit mind the might which I behold;
But soon in me shall Loneliness renew

---

¹ the bones of the French killed at the battle of Morat remained for ages after, heaped in a pyramid on the field.
² the regions beyond the Styx, a fabled river over which the ancients believed the spirits or shades of men passed after death. The spirits of unburied bodies were obliged to wander on the bank of the river—the Stygian coast—for a hundred years before being carried over.
³ referring to the battle of Cannæ (a town of Italy), 216 B.C., in which the famous Carthaginian general, Hannibal, defeated the Romans.
⁴ extremely severe, like the laws of Draco (an ancient Anthenian lawmaker), which made death the punishment of every crime, great or small.
⁵ in Switzerland—also called Lake Geneva.

Thoughts hid, but not less cherished than of old,
Ere mingling with the herd¹ had penned me in their fold.

. . . .

LXXI.

Is it not better, then, to be alone,
And love Earth only for its earthly sake?
By the blue rushing of the arrowy Rhone,²
Or the pure bosom of its nursing lake,
Which feeds it as a mother who doth make
A fair but froward infant her own care,
Kissing its cries away as these awake;—
Is it not better thus our lives to wear,
Than join the crushing crowd, doomed to inflict or bear?

. . . .

LXXV.

Are not the mountains, waves, and skies a part
Of me and of my soul, as I of them?
Is not the love of these deep in my heart
With a pure passion? should I not contemn
All objects, if compared with these? and stem
A tide of suffering, rather than forego
Such feelings for the hard and worldly phlegm
Of those whose eyes are only turned below,
Gazing upon the ground, with thoughts which dare not glow?

LXXVI.

But this is not my theme; and I return
To that which is immediate, and require
Those who find contemplation in the urn,
To look on One³ whose dust was once all fire,

---
¹ society.
² a great river of Switzerland and France; it flows through the Lake of Geneva.
³ Rousseau (pron., *Roo-so*), a celebrated French writer and philosopher, born in Geneva, 1712.

A native of the land where I respire
The clear air for a while—a passing guest,
Where he became a being—whose desire
Was to be glorious; 'twas a foolish quest,
The which to gain and keep he sacrificed all rest.

LXXVII.

Here the self-torturing sophist,¹ wild Rousseau,
The apostle of affliction, he who threw
Enchantment over passion, and from woe
Wrung overwhelming eloquence, first drew
The breath which made him wretched; yet he knew
How to make madness beautiful, and cast
O'er erring deeds and thoughts a heavenly hue
Of words, like sunbeams, dazzling as they past
The eyes, which o'er them shed tears feelingly and fast.

. . . . . .

LXXXV.

Clear, placid Leman! thy contrasted lake,
With the wild world I dwelt in, is a thing
Which warns me, with its stillness, to forsake
Earth's troubled waters for a purer spring.
This quiet sail is as a noiseless wing
To waft me from distraction; once I loved
Torn ocean's roar, but thy soft murmuring
Sounds sweet as if a sister's voice reproved,
That I with stern delights should e'er have been so moved.

LXXXVI.

It is the hush of night, and all between
Thy margin and the mountains, dusk, yet clear.
Mellow'd and mingling, yet distinctly seen,
Save darkened Jura,² whose capt heights appear

---

¹ The sophists in ancient Greece were teachers of eloquence, philosophy, and politics.
² a range of mountains extending through parts of Switzerland, France, and Germany.

Precipitously steep; and drawing near,
There breathes a living fragrance from the shore,
Of flowers yet fresh with childhood; on the ear
Drops the light drip of the suspended oar,
Or chirps the grasshopper one good-night carol more;

LXXXVII.

He is an evening reveler, who makes
His life an infancy, and sings his fill;
At intervals, some bird from out the brakes
Starts into voice a moment, then is still.
There seems a floating whisper on the hill.
But that is fancy, for the starlight dews
All silently their tears of love instill,
Weeping themselves away, till they infuse
Deep into Nature's breast the spirit of her hues.[1]

LXXXVIII.

Ye stars! which are the poetry of heaven,
If in your bright leaves we would read the fate
Of men and empires—'tis to be forgiven,
That in our aspirations to be great,
Our destinies o'erleap their mortal state,
And claim a kindred with you; for ye are
A beauty and a mystery, and create
In us such love and reverence from afar,
That fortune, fame, power, life, have named themselves a star.

LXXXIX.

All heaven and earth are still—though not in sleep,
But breathless, as we grow when feeling most;
And silent, as we stand in thoughts too deep:
All heaven and earth are still: From the high host

---

[1] During his stay in Switzerland Byron resided in the village of Coligny, within view of Geneva. Every evening he had a sail on the lake, and to the feelings thus created we owe these delightful stanzas.

Of stars, to the lulled lake and mountain-coast,
All is concentred in a life intense,
Where not a beam, nor air, nor leaf is lost,
But hath a part of being, and a sense
Of that which is of all Creator and defence.

. . . . . .

XCII.

The sky is changed!—and such a change! Oh night,
And storm, and darkness, ye are wondrous strong,
Yet lovely in your strength, as is the light
Of a dark eye in woman! Far along,
From peak to peak, the rattling crags among,
Leaps the live thunder![1] Not from one lone cloud,
But every mountain now hath found a tongue;
And Jura answers, through her misty shroud,
Back to the joyous Alps, who call to her aloud!

XCIII.

And this is in the night:—Most glorious night!
Thou wert not sent for slumber! let me be
A sharer in thy fierce and far delight—
A portion of the tempest and of thee!
How the lit lake shines, a phosphoric sea,[2]
And the big rain comes dancing to the earth!
And now again 'tis black,—and now, the glee
Of the loud hills shakes with its mountain mirth,
As if they did rejoice o'er a young earthquake's birth.

. . . . . .

XCVIII.

The morn is up again, the dewy morn,
With breath all incense, and with cheek all bloom,
Laughing the clouds away with playful scorn,
And living as if earth contained no tomb,—

---

[1] referring to a great thunder-storm which occurred on the night of June 13, 1816.
[2] shining like phosphorus, a substance that gives forth a luminous vapor.

And glowing into day : we may resume
The march of our existence : and thus I,
Still on thy shores, fair Leman ! may find room
And food for meditation, nor pass by
Much, that may give us pause, if pondered fittingly.

  . . . . . .

C.

Clarens![1] by heavenly feet thy paths are trod—
Undying Love's, who here ascends a throne
To which the steps are mountains ; where the god[2]
Is a pervading life and light—so shown
Not on those summits solely, nor alone
In the still cave and forest ; o'er the flower
His eye is sparkling. and his breath hath blown.
His soft and summer breath, whose tender power
Passes the strength of storms in their most desolate hour

  . . . . . .

CV.

Lausanne ! and Ferney ![3] ye have been the abodes
Of names[4] which unto you bequeathed a name ;
Mortals, who sought and found, by dangerous roads,
A path to perpetuity of fame :
They were gigantic minds, and their steep aim
Was, Titan-like,[5] on daring doubts to pile
Thoughts[6] which should call down thunder, and the
  flame

[1] a village near Lake Geneva.   [2] of love.
[3] Lausanne and Ferney are towns of Switzerland.
[4] referring to Gibbon and Voltaire. Gibbon was author of the celebrated book, "The Decline and Fall of the Roman Empire." He resided for many years at Lausanne, and wrote a great part of his book there. Voltaire was a famous French writer. He spent the last twenty years of his life at Ferney.
[5] The Titans were powerful giants, or gods, of ancient Greek fable. They made war upon Jupiter, king of the gods. and in order to reach his palace, on the top of Mount Olympus (Greece), they piled mountain upon mountain, from which, however, they were hurled down by the thunderbolts of Jupiter.
[6] referring to the infidel teaching of some of the writings of Voltaire and Gibbon.

Of Heaven, again assailed, if Heaven the while
On man and man's research could deign do more than
    smile.

CVI.

The one [1] was fire and fickleness, a child
Most mutable in wishes, but in mind
A wit as various—gay, grave, sage, or wild,—
Historian, bard, philosopher combined :
He multiplied himself among mankind,
The Proteus [2] of their talents : But his own
Breathed most in ridicule,—which, as the wind,
Blew where it listed, laying all things prone,—
Now to o'erthrow a fool, and now to shake a throne.

CVII.

The other,[3] deep and slow, exhausting thought,
And hiving wisdom with each studious year,
In meditation dwelt, with learning wrought,
And shaped his weapon with an edge severe.
  .   .   .   .   .   .

CIX.

But let me quit man's works, again to read
His Maker's, spread around me, and suspend
This page, which from my reveries I feed,
Until it seems prolonging without end.
The clouds above me to the white Alps tend,
And I must pierce them, and survey whate'er
May be permitted, as my steps I bend
To their most great and growing region, where
The earth to her embrace compels the powers of air.

---

[1] Voltaire.
[2] a sea-god, according to the ancients, who had power to change himself instantaneously into different forms.
[3] Gibbon.

CX.

Italia!¹ too, Italia! looking on thee
Full flashes on the soul the light of ages,
Since the fierce Carthaginian ² almost won thee,
To the last halo of the chiefs and sages
Who glorify thy consecrated pages :
Thou wert the throne and grave of empires ;³ still,
The fount at which the panting mind assuages
Her thirst of knowledge, quaffing there her fill,
Flows from the eternal source of Rome's imperial hill.

CXI.

Thus far have I proceeded in a theme
Renewed with no kind auspices :—to feel
We are not what we have been, and to deem
We are not what we should be,—and to steel
The heart against itself : and to conceal,
With a proud caution, love or hate, or aught,—
Passion or feeling, purpose, grief, or zeal,—
Which is the tyrant spirit of our thought,
Is a stern task of soul :—No matter,—it is taught.

CXII.

And for these words, thus woven into song,
It may be that they are a harmless wile,—
The coloring of the scenes which fleet along,
Which I would seize, in passing, to beguile
My breast, or that of others, for a while.
Fame is the thirst of youth—but I am not
So young as to regard men's frown or smile
As loss or guerdon of a glorious lot :
I stood and stand alone—remembered or forgot.

. . . .

¹ Italy.
² Hannibal, the famous general of Carthage (North Africa), who, in 218 B.C., marching with a great army from Spain, crossed the Alps into Italy, and defeated the Romans in several battles.
³ referring to the many conquests and vast power of the ancient Romans.

CXV.

My daughter! with thy name this song begun—
My daughter! with thy name thus much shall end.
I see thee not, I hear thee not,—but none
Can be so wrapt in thee; thou art the friend
To whom the shadows of far years extend:
Albeit my brow thou never shouldst behold,
My voice shall with thy future visions blend,
And reach into thy heart,—when mine is cold—
A token and a tone, even from thy father's mold.

. . . . . .

CANTO THE FOURTH.

I.

I stood in Venice,[1] on the Bridge of Sighs;[2]
A palace and a prison on each hand:
I saw from out the wave her structures rise
As from the stroke of the enchanter's wand;
A thousand years their cloudy wings expand
Around me, and a dying Glory smiles
O'er the far times when many a subject land
Looked to the winged Lion's[3] marble piles,
Where Venice sate in state, throned on her hundred isles!

II.

She looks a sea Cybele,[4] fresh from ocean,
Rising with her tiara of proud towers

---

[1] a beautiful city of Italy, built on a cluster of small islands at the northwest point of the Adriatic Sea. Most of the streets are canals, on which passengers are conveyed in light boats called gondolas.

[2] in former times, when Venice was a great and powerful republic, the governor or president was called the Doge. The communication between the ancient palace of the Doges and the prisons of Venice is by a gloomy bridge, or covered gallery, over which prisoners condemned to death were led to be executed, hence the bridge is known as the Bridge of Sighs.

[3] The Lion of St. Mark was the standard or national emblem of the Venetian Republic, St. Mark being the patron saint, and the figure of a lion being among the decorations of St. Mark's Cathedral (Venice), one of the most beautiful churches in the world.

[4] (pron. sib'e-lee) the mother of Jupiter and many of the other gods.

At airy distance, with majestic motion,
A ruler of the waters and their powers;
And such she was; her daughters had their dowers
From spoils of nations, and the exhaustless East
Poured in her lap all gems in sparkling showers.[1]
In purple was she robed, and of her feast
Monarchs partook and deemed their dignity increased.

III.

In Venice, Tasso's echoes[2] are no more,
And silent rows the songless gondolier;
Her palaces are crumbling to the shore,
And music meets not always now the ear;
These days are gone—but beauty still is here.
States fall, arts fade—but Nature doth not die,
Nor yet forget how Venice once was dear,
The pleasant place of all festivity,
The revel of the earth, the mask[3] of Italy!

IV.

But unto us she hath a spell beyond
Her name in story, and her long array
Of mighty shadows, whose dim forms despond
Above the dogeless city's vanished sway;
Ours is a trophy which will not decay
With the Rialto;[4] Shylock[5] and the Moor,[6]
And Pierre,[7] can not be swept or worn away—

---

[1] referring to the extensive trade and commerce at one time carried on by Venice with eastern countries—Syria, Egypt, India, etc.

[2] Tasso was a great Italian poet (born 1544). From one of his poems, "Jerusalem Delivered," parts of the song of the gondoliers (Venetian boat rowers) were taken.

[3] a festive entertainment; meaning here the chief place of pleasure in Italy.

[4] name of one of the numerous bridges in Venice.

[5] the Jew in Shakespeare's play, "The Merchant of Venice," in which the Rialto is also mentioned.

[6] the principal character in Shakespeare's play of "Othello," the scene of which is partly in Venice.

[7] a character represented as a patriot in the play of "Venice Preserved," written by Thomas Otway, an English dramatic poet of the seventeenth century.

The keystones of the arch ! though all were o'er,
For us repeopled were the solitary shore.

V.

The beings of the mind are not of clay ;
Essentially immortal, they create
And multiply in us a brighter ray
And more beloved existence : that which Fate
Prohibits to dull life, in this our state
Of mortal bondage, by these spirits supplied,
First exiles, then replaces what we hate ;
Watering the heart whose early flowers have died,
And with a fresher growth replenishing the void.

VI.

Such is the refuge of our youth and age,
The first from Hope, the last from Vacancy ;
And this worn feeling peoples many a page,
And, may be, that which grows beneath mine eye.
Yet there are things whose strong reality
Outshines our fairy-land : in shape and hues
More beautiful than our fantastic sky,
And the strange constellations which the Muse
O'er her wild universe is skillful to diffuse :

VII.

I saw or dreamed of such,—but let them go—
They came like truth, and disappeared like dreams :
And whatsoe'er they were—are now but so ;
I could replace them if I would : still teems
My mind with many a form which aptly seems
Such as I sought for, and at moments found ;
Let these too go—for waking Reason deems
Such overweening phantasies unsound,
And other voices speak, and other sights surround.

. . . . . .

XI.

The spouseless Adriatic mourns her lord :
And, annual marriage now no more renewed,[1]
The Bucentaur lies rotting unrestored,
Neglected garment of her widowhood !
St. Mark yet sees his lion [2] where he stood
Stand, but in mockery of his withered power,
Over the proud place where an Emperor sued : [3]
And monarchs gazed and envied in the hour
When Venice was a queen with an unequaled dower.

. . . .

XVIII.

I loved her from my boyhood ; she to me
Was as a fairy city of the heart,
Rising like water-columns from the sea,
Of joy the sojourn, and of wealth the mart.
And Otway, Radcliffe, Schiller, Shakespeare's [4] art,
Had stamped her image in me, and even so,
Although I found her thus, we did not part,
Perchance even dearer in her day of woe,
Than when she was a boast, a marvel, and a show.

. . . .

XXV.

But my soul wanders : I demand it back
To meditate amongst decay, and stand

---

[1] In former times there used to be in Venice every year, on Ascension Thursday (fortieth day after Easter), a grand water-procession, formed of a number of the citizens, in gondolas, headed by the Doge in a vessel called the *Bucentaur*, which was kept specially for the purpose. When the procession reached the mouth of one of the channels opening into the sea, the Doge "married the Adriatic," by dropping a ring into the water, at the same time repeating the words, "We wed thee with this ring in token of our true and perpetual sovereignty."

[2] See note 3, page 108.

[3] Frederick I., Emperor of Germany from 1152 to 1190, who was excommunicated by Pope Alexander III., with whom he had a quarrel for many years. In 1177 Frederick submitted to Alexander, and appeared before him in St. Mark's Cathedral, Venice, where the excommunication was removed.

[4] names of authors who wrote about Venice.

A ruin amidst ruins; there to track
Fall'n states and buried greatness, o'er a land
Which *was* the mightiest in its old command,
And *is* the loveliest, and must ever be
The master-mold of Nature's heavenly hand,
Wherein were cast the heroic and the free,
The beautiful, the brave—the lords of earth and sea.

XXVI.

The commonwealth of kings, the men of Rome!
And even since, and now, fair Italy!
Thou art the garden of the world, the home
Of all Art yields, and Nature can decree;
Even in thy desert, what is like to thee?
Thy very weeds are beautiful, thy waste
More rich than other climes' fertility;
Thy wreck a glory, and thy ruin graced
With an immaculate charm which can not be defaced.

XXVII.

The moon is up, and yet it is not night—
Sunset divides the sky with her—a sea
Of glory streams along the Alpine height
Of blue Friuli's [1] mountains; Heaven is free
From clouds, but of all the colors seems to be—
Melted to one vast Iris [2] of the West,
Where the Day joins the past Eternity;
While, on the other hand, meek Dian's crest [3]
Floats through the azure air—an island of the blest!

XXVIII.

A single star is at her side, and reigns
With her o'er half the lovely heaven; but still

---

[1] Friuli, a district in North Italy.
[2] the goddess supposed to have been the representative of the rainbow.
[3] the moon. Dian or Diana was the goddess of the moon.

Yon sunny sea heaves brightly, and remains
Rolled o'er the peak of the far Rhætian hill,[1]
As Day and Night contending were, until
Nature reclaimed her order :—gently flows
The deep-dyed Brenta,[2] where their hues instill
The odorous purple of a new-born rose,
Which streams upon her stream, and glassed within it
   glows,

XXIX.

Filled with the face of heaven, which, from afar,
Comes down upon the waters ; all its hues,
From the rich sunset to the rising star,
Their magical variety diffuse :
And now they change ; a paler shadow strews
Its mantle o'er the mountains ; parting day
Dies like the dolphin, whom each pang imbues
With a new color as it gasps away,[3]
The last still loveliest, till—'tis gone—and all is gray.

. . . . . .

XXXV.

Ferrara ![4] in thy wide and grass-grown streets,
Whose symmetry was not for solitude,
There seems as 'twere a curse upon the seats
Of former sovereigns, and the antique brood
Of Este,[5] which for many an age made good
Its strength within thy walls, and was of yore
Patron or tyrant, as the changing mood

---

[1] Rhætia, the ancient name of a district north of Italy, including part of the Alps.
[2] a river in the north of Italy flowing into the Gulf of Venice.
[3] The dolphin is a large fish celebrated for its changes of color when dying.
[4] a city in the north of Italy.
[5] an old and powerful family of Italy, which, in the thirteenth century, obtained possession of Ferrara.

8

Of petty power impelled, of those¹ who wore
The wreath which Dante's² brow alone had worn before.

XXXVI.

And Tasso is their glory and their shame.
Hark to his strain! and then survey his cell!
And see how dearly earned Torquato's³ fame,
And where Alfonso⁴ bade his poet dwell.
The miserable despot could not quell
The insulted mind he sought to quench, and blend
With the surrounding maniacs, in the hell
Where he had plunged it. Glory without end
Scattered the clouds away—and on that name⁵ attend

XXXVII.

The tears and praises of all time, while thine
Would rot in its oblivion—in the sink
Of worthless dust, which from thy boasted line
Is shaken into nothing; but the link
Thou formest in his fortunes bids us think
Of thy poor malice, naming thee with scorn—
Alfonso! how thy ducal pageants shrink
From thee! if in another station born,
Scarce fit to be the slave of him thou mad'st to mourn.

. . . . . .

XXXIX.

Peace to Torquato's injured shade! 'twas his
In life and death to be the mark where Wrong

---

¹ poets and literary men, who were much patronized by the Este family.
² Dante, the greatest of Italian poets, was born in Florence in 1265. His chief work is the "Divina Commedia" (Divine Comedy), describing a vision in which the poet is conducted through Hell and Purgatory, and then through Heaven, where he beholds God.
³ Torquato Tasso, the Italian poet.
⁴ Alfonso, Duke of Ferrara, who put the poet Tasso in prison, with the purpose, it is said, of keeping him under restraint while suffering from insanity.
⁵ Tasso.

Aimed with her poisoned arrows—but to miss.
Oh, victor unsurpassed in modern song!
Each year brings forth its millions: but how long
The tide of generations shall roll on,
And not the whole combined and countless throng
Compose a mind like thine? Though all in one
Condensed their scattered rays, they would not form a sun.

XL.

Great as thou art, yet paralleled by those
Thy countrymen, before thee born to shine,
The bards of Hell and Chivalry:¹ first rose
The Tuscan father's² comedy divine;
Then, not unequal to the Florentine,³
The Southern Scott,⁴ the minstrel who called forth
A new creation with his magic line,
And, like the Ariosto of the North,
Sang ladye-love and war, romance and knightly worth.

. . . .

XLVIII.

But Arno⁵ wins us to the fair white walls,
Where the Etrurian Athens⁶ claims and keeps
A softer feeling for her fairy halls.
Girt by her theater of hills, she reaps
Her corn, and wine, and oil, and Plenty leaps
To laughing life, with her redundant horn.⁷
Along the banks where smiling Arno sweeps,

---

¹ Dante and Ariosto. The latter was born at Reggio in 1474.
² Dante is so called, the place of his birth (Florence) being in the province of Tuscany.
³ Dante.
⁴ Ariosto is here meant. He is called "the Southern Scott" because his great poem, "Orlando Furioso," treats of "ladye-love and war," like some of those of the famous Scottish poet (Scott), and in the second next line the latter is referred to as the "Ariosto of the North."
⁵ a river of Tuscany (central Italy) flowing into the Mediterranean.
⁶ Florence (on the Arno), situated in the district anciently named Etruria, and in former times almost as celebrated as Athens for works of art and learning.
⁷ Ceres, the goddess of Agriculture, was represented as bearing in her hand a "horn of plenty," pouring its abundant contents of fruits and flowers on the ground.

Was modern Luxury of Commerce born,
And buried Learning rose, redeemed to a new morn.

XLIX.

There, too, the Goddess loves in stone,[1] and fills
The air around with beauty; we inhale
The ambrosial[2] aspect, which, beheld, instills
Part of its immortality; the veil
Of heaven is half undrawn; within the pale
We stand, and in that form and face behold
What Mind can make, when Nature's self would fail;
And to the fond idolaters of old
Envy the innate flash which such a soul could mold:

. . . . . .

LIV.

In Santa Croce's[3] holy precincts lie
Ashes which make it holier, dust which is
E'en in itself an immortality,
Though there were nothing save the past, and this
The particle of those sublimities
Which have relapsed to chaos:—here repose
Angelo's,[4] Alfieri's[5] bones, and his,
The starry Galileo,[6] with his woes;
Here Machiavelli's[7] earth returned to whence it rose.

LV.

These are four minds, which, like the elements,
Might furnish forth creation:—Italy!

---

[1] referring to the statue of the goddess Venus in Florence, famed for its artistic excellence and beauty, and known as the Venus de Medici, from having been preserved for a time in the palace of the Medici family in Rome. The statue is the work of Cleomenes, an Athenian sculptor of the second century before Christ.

[2] *adj.*, from ambrosia, the food of the gods, which rendered those who partook of it immortal.

[3] Santa Croce, the Cathedral of Florence.

[4] Michael Angelo, one of Italy's greatest sculptors and painters, born 1474.

[5] Count Alfieri, Italian dramatic poet, born 1749.

[6] Galileo Galilei, famous astronomer, born at Pisa (north Italy), 1564; imprisoned in Rome for teaching the revolution of the earth round the sun.

[7] Nicholas Machiavelli, statesman and writer, born in Florence, 1469.

Time, which hath wronged thee with ten thousand rents
Of thine imperial garment, shall deny,
And hath denied, to every other sky,
Spirits which soar from ruin :—thy decay
Is still impregnate with divinity,
Which gilds it with revivifying ray ;
Such as the great of yore, Canova[1] is to-day.

LVI.

But where repose the all Etruscan three—
Dante, and Petrarch,[2] and, scarce less than they,
The Bard of Prose, creative spirit ! he
Of the Hundred Tales of love[3]—where did they lay
Their bones, distinguished from our common clay
In death as life ? Are they resolved to dust,
And have their country's marbles nought to say ?
Could not her quarries furnish forth one bust ?
Did they not to her breast their filial earth entrust ?

LVII.

Ungrateful Florence ! Dante sleeps afar,[4]
Like Scipio,[5] buried by the upbraiding shore ;
Thy factions, in their worse than civil war,
Proscribed the bard [6] whose name for evermore
Their children's children would in vain adore
With the remorse of ages : and the crown
Which Petrarch's laureate brow supremely wore,[7]

---

[1] Antonio Canova, a great sculptor, born in north Italy 1757, died 1822.
[2] celebrated Italian poet, born at Arezzo, 1304.
[3] referring to the "Decameron," a book of one hundred stories, written by Boccaccio (*pron.* bok-kat′cho), who was born in Paris, in 1313, of Italian parentage. Dante, Petrarch, and Boccaccio are called "Etruscan," because their families belonged to the district of Etruria, the inhabitants of which were called Etruscans.
[4] buried at Ravenna, central Italy.
[5] Publius Cornelius Scipio, a famous general of ancient Rome, born 237 B.C. ; buried, it is said, near the sea-shore at Liternum, Campania, south Italy.
[6] referring to the banishment of Dante from Florence by one of the factions at the time in control of the city.
[7] Petrarch was crowned with a poet's laurel wreath in the Capitol at Rome in 1341.

Upon a far and foreign soil had grown.
His life, his fame, his grave,[1] though rifled—not thine own.

LVIII.

Boccaccio to his parent earth bequeathed
His dust,—and lies it not her Great among,
With many a sweet and solemn requiem breathed
O'er him who formed the Tuscan's siren[2] tongue ?
That music in itself, whose sounds are song,
The poetry of speech ? No:—even his tomb
Uptorn, must bear the hyæna bigot's wrong,[3]
No more amidst the meaner dead find room,
Nor claim a passing sigh, because it told for *whom!*

. . . .

LXXVIII.

O Rome ! my country ! city of the soul !
The orphans of the heart must turn to thee.
Lone mother of dead empires ! and control
In their shut breasts their petty misery.
What are our woes and sufferance ? Come and see
The cypress, hear the owl, and plod your way
O'er steps of broken thrones and temples, Ye !
Whose agonies are evils of a day—
A world is at our feet as fragile as our clay.[4]

LXXIX.

The Niobe[5] of nations ! there she stands,
Childless and crownless in her voiceless woe ;

---

[1] at Arqua, in north Italy.

[2] musical, the language of Tuscany being remarkable for its sweetness and softness.

[3] Boccaccio was buried in a church in Certaldo (central Italy), from which his remains were afterwards ejected by persons who disliked some of his writings.

[4] In a letter from Rome, shortly after his arrival in the city. Byron wrote : " I have been some days in Rome the Wonderful. I am delighted with Rome. As a whole—ancient and modern—it beats Greece, Constantinople, everything—at least that I have ever seen."

[5] Niobe, wife of Amphion, an ancient Greek king. She had twelve children, of whom she was so proud that she despised Latona, who had only two—the god Apollo and the goddess Diana. To punish her pride the two deities killed all her children, at which she was struck dumb with grief ; and the other gods, pitying her distress, changed her into stone.

An empty urn within her withered hands,
Whose holy dust was scattered long ago;
The Scipios'[1] tomb contains no ashes now;
The very sepulchers lie tenantless
Of their heroic dwellers : dost thou flow,
Old Tiber![2] through a marble wilderness?
Rise, with thy yellow waves, and mantle her distress!

LXXX.

The Goth,[3] the Christian, Time. War, Flood, and Fire,
Have dealt upon the seven-hilled city's[4] pride :
She saw her glories star by star expire,
And up the steep barbarian monarchs ride,
Where the car[5] climbed the Capitol : far and wide
Temple and tower went down, nor left a site ;—
Chaos of ruins! who shall trace the void,
O'er the dim fragments cast a lunar light,
And say, "Here was, or is." where all is doubly night?

LXXXI.

The double night of ages, and of her,
Night's daughter, Ignorance, hath wrapt, and wrap
All round us; we but feel our way to err :
The ocean hath its chart, the stars their map;
And Knowledge spreads them on her ample lap;
But Rome is as the desert, where we steer
Stumbling o'er recollections : now we clap
Our hands, and cry, "Eureka!"[6] it is clear—
When but some false mirage of ruin rises near.

[1] an illustrious family of ancient Rome.
[2] the river which flows through Rome. Its water has a yellowish tint from the color o.· the earth or mud it washes in its course.
[3] The Goths, a fierce tribe of northern Europe, invaded Italy in the fifth century, under their king, Alaric, and captured and pillaged Rome.
[4] Rome, built on seven hills.
[5] Roman generals who won great victories were honored by triumphs, or grand processions, through the streets of the city to the Capitol, in which the victor sat in a car or chariot drawn by four horses.
[6] Greek word for "I have found it."

LXXXII.

Alas! the lofty city! and alas!
The trebly hundred triumphs! and the day
When Brutus[1] made the dagger's edge surpass
The conqueror's sword in bearing fame away!
Alas for Tully's[2] voice, and Virgil's[3] lay,
And Livy's[4] pictured page! But these shall be
Her resurrection; all beside—decay.
Alas for Earth, for never shall we see
That brightness in her eye she bore when Rome was free!

. . . . . .

CXXVIII.

Arches on arches! as it were that Rome,
Collecting the chief trophies of her line,
Would build up all her triumphs in one dome,
Her Coliseum[5] stands; the moonbeams shine
As 'twere its natural torches, for divine
Should be the light which streams here, to illume
This long explored but still exhaustless mine
Of contemplation; and the azure gloom
Of an Italian night, where the deep skies assume

CXXIX.

Hues which have words, and speak to ye of heaven,
Floats o'er this vast and wondrous monument,
And shadows forth its glory. There is given
Unto the things of earth, which Time hath bent,
A spirit's feeling, and where he hath leant
His hand, but broke his scythe, there is a power
And magic in the ruined battlement,

---

[1] Marcus Junius Brutus, who killed Julius Cæsar, 44 B.C.

[2] Tully, Marcus Tullius Cicero, the greatest orator of ancient Rome, born 106 B.C.

[3] Virgil, the greatest of Roman poets, born 70 B.C.

[4] Livy, the greatest of Roman historians, born 61 B.C.

[5] a vast theatre in Rome, covering five acres of ground, and capable of containing eighty-seven thousand persons, finished by the Emperor Titus in 80 A.D.

For which the palace of the present hour
Must yield its pomp, and wait till ages are its dower.

. . . . . .

CXXXIX.

And here the buzz of eager nations ran,
In murmured pity, or loud-roared applause,
As man was slaughtered by his fellow-man.[1]
And wherefore slaughtered? wherefore, but because
Such were the bloody Circus' genial laws,
And the imperial pleasure.[2] Wherefore not?
What matters where we fall to fill the maws
Of worms—on battle-plains or listed spot?
Both are but theatres where the chief actors rot.

CXL.

I see before me the Gladiator lie:
He leans upon his hand—his manly brow
Consents to death, but conquers agony,
And his drooped head sinks gradually low—
And through his side the last drops, ebbing slow
From the red gash, fall heavy, one by one,
Like the first of a thunder-shower; and now
The arena[3] swims around him—he is gone,
Ere ceased the inhuman shout which hailed the wretch
who won.

CXLI.

He heard it, but he heeded not—his eyes
Were with his heart, and that was far away;

---

[1] In the Coliseum gladiators fought with one another or with wild beasts for the amusement of the spectators. The gladiators were generally slaves, bought or captured in war, and trained for this purpose. They were compelled to fight to death, and if any showed cowardice he was killed. The Emperor Trajan gave a show of one hundred and twenty-three days, in which two thousand men fought with one another and with wild beasts for the entertainment of seventy thousand Romans.

[2] at the pleasure of the emperor and citizens.

[3] the open space in the centre, where the performance took place, so called from being covered with sand, the Latin word for which is *arena*.

He reck'd not of the life he lost nor prize,
But where his rude hut by the Danube[1] lay,
There were his young barbarians[2] all at play,
There was their Dacian[3] mother—he, their sire,
Butchered to make a Roman holiday—
All this rush'd with his blood—Shall he expire,
And unavenged?—Arise! ye Goths, and glut your ire!

CXLII.

But here, where Murder breathed her bloody steam;
And here, where buzzing nations choked the ways,
And roared and murmured like a mountain stream
Dashing or winding as its torrent strays;
Here, where the Roman million's blame or praise
Was death or life, the playthings of a crowd,
My voice sounds much—and fall the stars' faint rays
On the arena void—seats crushed, walls bowed—
And galleries where my steps seem echoes strangely loud.

CXLIII.

A ruin—yet what ruin! from its mass
Wall, palaces, half-cities, have been reared;
Yet oft the enormous skeleton ye pass,
And marvel where the spoil could have appeared.
Hath it indeed been plundered, or but cleared?
Alas! developed, opens the decay,
When the colossal fabric's form is neared;
It will not bear the brightness of the day,
Which streams too much on all years, man, have reft away.

CXLIV.

But when the rising moon begins to climb
Its topmost arch, and gently pauses there;

---

[1] river of central Europe.   [2] his children.
[3] Dacia, a country of central Europe, conquered by the Emperor Trajan.

When the stars twinkle through the loops of time,
And the low night-breeze waves along the air,
The garland forest, which the gray walls wear,
Like laurels on the bald first Cæsar's head ;[1]
When the light shines serene, but doth not glare,
Then in this magic circle raise the dead :
Heroes have trod this spot—'tis on their dust ye tread.

CXLV.

" While stands the Coliseum, Rome shall stand :
When falls the Coliseum, Rome shall fall ;
And when Rome falls—the World."[2] From our own land
Thus spake the pilgrims o'er this mighty wall
In Saxon times, which we are wont to call
Ancient ; and these three mortal things are still
On their foundations, and unaltered all ;
Rome and her Ruin past Redemption's skill,
The World, the same wide den—of thieves, or what ye will

CXLVI.

Simple, erect, severe, austere, sublime—
Shrine of all saints and temple of all gods,
From Jove to Jesus—spared and blest by time ;
Looking tranquillity, while falls or nods
Arch, empire, each thing round thee, and man plods
His way through thorns to ashes—glorious dome !
Shalt thou not last ?—Time's scythe and tyrants' rods
Shiver upon thee—sanctuary and home
Of art and piety—Pantheon ![3]—pride of Rome !

---

[1] Julius Cæsar, being bald, wore a laurel wreath on his head when he appeared in the Roman Senate.

[2] these words, used by Anglo-Saxon pilgrims who visited Rome in the end of the seventh century, are quoted from Gibbon's " Decline and Fall of the Roman Empire," and are taken as a proof '..at at that time the Coliseum was entire.

[3] a magnificent te..ple dedicated to all the gods, erected in 27 B.C., and the only ancient Roman edifice that remains entirely preserved. It is lighted by one aperture in the centre of the dome. It has been made the receptacle of busts of distinguished men of modern times.

CXLVII.

Relic of nobler days, and noblest arts!
Despoiled yet perfect, with thy circle spreads
A holiness appealing to all hearts—
To art a model; and to him who treads
Rome for the sake of ages, Glory sheds
Her light through thy sole aperture; to those
Who worship, here are altars for their beads;
And they who feel for genius may repose
Their eyes on honored forms, whose busts around them close.

. . . . . .

CLIII.

But lo! the dome—the vast and wondrous dome,[1]
To which Diana's marvel[2] was a cell—
Christ's mighty shrine above his martyr's[3] tomb!
I have beheld the Ephesian's miracle[2]—
Its columns strew the wilderness, and dwell
The hyæna and the jackal in their shade;
I have beheld Sophia's bright roofs[4] swell
Their glittering mass i' the sun, and have surveyed
Its sanctuary the while the usurping Moslem prayed;

CLIV.

But thou, of temples old, or altars new,
Standest alone—with nothing like to thee—
Worthiest of God, the holy and the true,
Since Zion's[5] desolation, when that He[6]

---

[1] the dome of St. Peter's, the largest and most magnificent church in the world.

[2] the temple of the goddess Diana at Ephesus (Asia Minor), one of the seven wonders of the world in ancient times.

[3] the Apostle St. Peter, said to have been martyred in Rome.

[4] St. Sophia, in Constantinople (Turkey), formerly a Christian church, now a Moslem or Mohammedan mosque.

[5] Zion, meaning the temple of Jerusalem.   [6] God.

Forsook His former city, what could be,
Of earthly structures, in His honor piled,
Of a sublimer aspect ? Majesty,
Power, Glory, Strength, and Beauty, all are aisled
In this eternal ark of worship undefiled.

. . . .

CLXXV.

But I forget.—My Pilgrim's shrine is won
And he [1] and I must part,—so let it be,—
His task and mine alike are nearly done ;
Yet once more let us look upon the sea :
The midland ocean [2] breaks on him and me,
And from the Alban Mount [3] we now behold
Our friend of youth, that Ocean, which when we
Beheld it last by Calpe's rock [4] unfold
Those waves, we followed on till the dark Euxine [5] rolled.

. . . . . .

CLXXVIII.

There is a pleasure in the pathless woods,
There is a rapture on the lonely shore,
There is society where none intrudes,
By the deep Sea, and music in its roar !
I love not Man the less, but Nature more,
From these our interviews, in which I steal
From all I may be, or have been before,
To mingle with the Universe, and feel
What I can ne'er express, yet cannot all conceal.

CLXXIX.

Roll on, thou deep and dark blue Ocean—roll !
Ten thousand fleets sweep over thee in vain ;
Man marks the earth with ruin—his control
Stops with the shore ; upon the watery plain

---

[1] Childe Harold.   [2] the Mediterranean Sea.
[3] some miles south of Rome.   [4] Gibraltar.   [5] the Black Sea.

The wrecks are all thy deed—nor doth remain
A shadow of man's ravage, save his own,
When for a moment, like a drop of rain,
He sinks into thy depths with bubbling groan,
Without a grave, unknelled,[1] uncoffined, and unknown.

CLXXX.

His steps are not upon thy paths—thy fields
Are not a spoil for him,—thou dost arise
And shake him from thee ; the vile strength he wields
For earth's destruction thou dost all despise,
Spurning him from thy bosom to the skies,
And send'st him, shivering in thy playful spray
And howling, to his gods, where haply lies
His petty hope in some near port or bay,
And dashest him again to earth :—there let him lay.

CLXXXI.

The armaments which thunder-strike the walls
Of rock-built cities, bidding nations quake,
And monarchs tremble in their capitals.
The oak leviathans,[2] whose huge ribs make
Their clay creator[3] the vain title take
Of lord of thee,[4] and arbiter of war ;
These are thy toys, and, as the snowy flake,
They melt into thy yeast of waves, which mar
Alike the Armada's[5] pride, or spoils of Trafalgar.[6]

CLXXXII.

Thy shores[7] are empires, changed in all save thee—
Assyria, Greece, Rome, Carthage, what are they ?

---

[1] without sound of funeral bell.
[2] great ships. The leviathan is mentioned in Scripture as a large sea animal.
[3] man.　　　　　[4] the ocean.
[5] Armada is the name given to the great fleet with which the Spaniards attempted to invade England in 1588.
[6] See note 4, page 72.　　　　　[7] of the Mediterranean.

Thy waters washed them power while they were free
And many a tyrant since : their shores obey
The stranger, slave, or savage ; their decay
Has dried up realms to deserts : not so thou,
Unchangeable save to thy wild wave's play—
Time writes no wrinkle on thine azure brow—
Such as creation's dawn beheld, thou rollest now.

CLXXXIII.

Thou glorious mirror,[1] where the Almighty's form
Glasses itself in tempests ; in all time,
Calm or convulsed—in breeze, or gale, or storm,
Icing the pole, or in the torrid clime
Dark-heaving ;—boundless, endless, and sublime—
The image of Eternity—the throne
Of the Invisible, even from out thy slime
The monsters of the deep are made ; each zone
Obeys thee : thou goest forth, dread, fathomless, alone.

CLXXXIV.

And I have loved thee, Ocean ! and my joy
Of youthful sports was on thy breast to be
Borne like thy bubbles, onward : from a boy
I wanton'd with thy breakers—they to me
Were a delight ; and if the freshening sea
Made them a terror—'twas a pleasing fear,
For I was as it were a child of thee,
And trusted to thy billows far and near,
And laid my hand upon thy mane [2]—as I do here.

CLXXXV.

My task is done—my song hath ceased—my theme
Has died into an echo ; it is fit
The spell should break of this protracted dream.
The torch shall be extinguished which hath lit

[1] the ocean.   [2] foamy crest of the waves.

My midnight lamp—and what is writ, is writ—
Would it were worthier! but I am not now
That which I have been—and my visions flit
Less palpably before me—and the glow
Which in my spirit dwelt is fluttering, faint, and low.

CLXXXVI.

Farewell! a word that must be, and hath been—
A sound which makes us linger;—yet,—farewell!
Ye, who have traced the Pilgrim to the scene
Which is his last, if in your memories dwell
A thought which once was his, if on ye swell
A single recollection, not in vain
He wore his sandal-shoon [1] and scallop-shell; [2]
Farewell! with *him* alone may rest the pain,
If such there were—with *you,* the moral of his strain.

[1] shoes formed of soles fastened to the feet; they were worn by pilgrims.
[2] a kind of shell found on the coast of Palestine, and worn by pilgrims to show that they had visited the Holy Land.

• Standard • Literature • Series •

Works of standard authors for supplementary reading in schools—complete selections or abridgments—with introductions and explanatory notes. Single numbers, 64 to 128 pages, stiff paper sides 12½ cents, cloth 20 cents; double numbers, 160 to 224 pages, stiff paper sides 20 cents, cloth 30 cents.

CONTENTS OF THE FIRST TWENTY-FOUR (24) NUMBERS, ARRANGED BY COUNTRIES AND AUTHORS

Starred numbers are DOUBLE. All the works are complete, or contain complete selections, except those marked "abr."

American Authors

COOPER—*The Spy,* No. 1, single (abr.), 128 pp.   *The Pilot, No. 2 (abr.), 181 pp.   *The Deerslayer, No. 8 (abr.), 160 pp.

DANA, R. H., Jr.—*Two Years Before the Mast,* No. 19 (abr.), 173 pp.

HAWTHORNE—*Twice-Told Tales,* No. 15, single, complete selections, 128 pp.: The Village Uncle, The Ambitious Guest, Mr. Higginbotham's Catastrophe, A Rill from the Town Pump, The Great Carbuncle, David Swan, Dr. Heidegger's Experiment, Peter Goldthwaite's Treasure, The Threefold Destiny, Old Esther Dudley.

A Wonder-Book, for Girls and Boys, No. 16, single, complete selections, 121 pp.: The Golden Touch, The Paradise of Children, The Three Golden Apples, The Miraculous Pitcher.

The Snow-Image and other Twice-Told Tales, No. 20, single, complete selections, 121 pp.: The Snow-Image, The Great Stone Face, Little Daffydowndilly, The Vision of the Fountain, The Seven Vagabonds, Little Annie's Ramble, The Prophetic Pictures.

IRVING—*The Alhambra,* No. 4, single, complete selections, 128 pp.: Palace of the Alhambra; Alhamar, the Founder of the Alhambra; Yusef Abul Hagig, the Finisher of the Alhambra; Panorama from the Tower of Comares; Legend of the Moor's Legacy; Legend of the Rose of the Alhambra; The Governor and the Notary; Governor Manco and the Soldier; Legend of Two Discreet Statues; Legend of Don Munio Sancho de Hinojosa; The Legend of the Enchanted Soldier.

The Sketch-Book, No. 17, single, complete selections, 121 pp.: The Author's Account of Himself, The Broken Heart, The Spectre Bridegroom, Rural Life in England, The Angler, John Bull, The Christmas Dinner, Stratford-on-Avon.

Knickerbocker Stories, No. 23, single, complete selections, 140 pp.: I. Broek, or the Dutch Paradise; II. From Knickerbocker's New York, (a) New Amsterdam under Van Twiller, (b) How William the Testy Defended the City, (c) Peter Stuyvesant's Voyage up the Hudson; III. Wolfert's Roost; IV. The Storm Ship; V. Rip Van Winkle; VI. A Legend of Sleepy Hollow.

Standard ✦ Literature ✦ Series

KENNEDY, J. P.—*Horse-Shoe Robinson, a Tale of the Revolution, No. 10 (abr.), 192 pp.

LONGFELLOW—Evangeline, a Tale of Acadie, No. 21, single, complete, 102 pp.

English Authors

BULWER-LYTTON—*Harold, the Last of the Saxon Kings, No. 12 (abr.), 160 pp.

BYRON—The Prisoner of Chillon and Other Poems, No. 11, single, complete selections, 128 pp.: The Prisoner of Chillon, Mazeppa, Childe Harold.

DICKENS—Christmas Stories, No. 5, single (abr.), 142 pp.: A Christmas Carol, The Cricket on the Hearth, The Child's Dream of a Star.
    Little Nell (from Old Curiosity Shop), No. 22, single (abr.), 123 pp.
    Paul Dombey (from Dombey and Son), No. 14, single (abr.), 128 pp.

SCOTT—*Ivanhoe, No. 24 (abr.), 180 pp. *Kenilworth, No. 7 (abr.), 164 pp. *Lady of the Lake, No. 9, complete, 192 pp. Rob Roy, No. 3, single (abr.), 130 pp.

SWIFT—Gulliver's Travels, Voyages to Lilliput and Brobdingnag, No. 13, single (abr.), 128 pp.

TENNYSON—Enoch Arden and Other Poems, No. 6, single, complete selections, 110 pp.: Enoch Arden; The Coming of Arthur; The Passing of Arthur; Columbus; The May Queen; New Year's Eve; Conclusion; Dora; The Charge of the Light Brigade; The Defence of Lucknow; Lady Clare; Break, Break, Break; The Brook; Bugle Song; Widow and Child; The Days That Are No More; I Envy Not; Oh, Yet We Trust; Ring Out, Wild Bells; Crossing the Bar (Tennyson's last poem).

French Authors

HUGO, VICTOR—*Ninety-Three, No. 18 (abr.), 157 pp.

Grading.—For **History Classes:** Spy, Pilot, Deerslayer, Horse-Shoe Robinson, Knickerbocker Stories, Harold, Kenilworth, Rob Roy, Ivanhoe, Ninety-Three, Alhambra. **Geography:** Two Years Before the Mast. **English Literature:** Evangeline, Lady of the Lake, Enoch Arden, Prisoner of Chillon, Sketch-Book. **Lower Grammar Grades:** Christmas Stories, Little Nell, Paul Dombey, Gulliver's Travels, Twice-Told Tales. **Primary Grades:** Wonder-Book, Snow-Image.

Numbers 25 to 40

Each with Introduction and Notes. Starred numbers, double.

25. ROBINSON CRUSOE. Defoe. Illustrated. For Young Readers.
*26. POEMS OF KNIGHTLY ADVENTURE. Tennyson, Arnold, Macaulay, Lowell. Four Complete Selections.

Standard ◆ Literature ◆ Series

*27. THE WATER WITCH. Cooper. With Map.
28. TALES OF A GRANDFATHER. Scott. Complete Selections.
*29. THE LAST OF THE MOHICANS. Cooper. With Map.
30. THE PILGRIM'S PROGRESS. Bunyan. For Young Readers.
*31. BLACK BEAUTY. Sewell. Complete.
*32. THE YEMASSEE. Cooper. With Map.
*33. WESTWARD HO! Kingsley. With Map.
*34. 'ROUND THE WORLD IN EIGHTY DAYS. Verne.
35. SWISS FAMILY ROBINSON. Wyss. Illustrated.
*36. THE CHILDHOOD OF DAVID COPPERFIELD. Dickens.
*37. THE SONG OF HIAWATHA. Longfellow. Complete.
*38. THE LAST DAYS OF POMPEII. Bulwer-Lytton.
39. FAIRY TALES. Second School Year. Selected Tales.
*40. THE LAY OF THE LAST MINSTREL. Scott. Complete.

WHAT PROMINENT EDUCATORS SAY

W. T. Harris, *Commissioner of Education, Washington, D. C.:* "I have examined very carefully one of the abridgments from Walter Scott, and I would not have believed the essentials of the story could have been retained with so severe an abridgment. But the story thus abridged has kept its interest and all of the chief threads of the plot. I am very glad that the great novels of Walter Scott are in course of publication by your house in such a form that school children, and older persons as yet unfamiliar with Walter Scott, may find an easy introduction. To read Walter Scott's novels is a large part of a liberal education, but his discourses on the history of the times and his disquisitions on motives render his stories too hard for the person of merely elementary education. But if one can interest himself in the plot, and skip these learned passages, he may, on a second reading, be able to grasp the whole novel. Hence I look to such abridgments as you have made for a great extension of Walter Scott's usefulness."

William H. Maxwell, *Superintendent of Public Instruction, New York City:* "I take great pleasure in commending to those who are seeking for good reading in the schools, the Standard Literature Series. The editors of the series have struck out a new line in the preparation of literature for schools. They have taken great works of fiction and poetry, and so edited them as to omit what is beyond the comprehension, or what would weary the attention, of children in the higher grades of elementary schools."

Standard ◆ Literature ◆ Series

Walter B. Gunnison, *Principal Erasmus Hall High School, Brooklyn, N. Y.* "I have watched with much interest the issues of the new Standard Literature Series, and have examined them all with care. I regard them as a distinct addition to the school literature of our country. The selections are admirable—the annotations clear and comprehensive, and the form convenient and artistic."

A. E. Winship, *Editor "Journal of Education," Boston, Mass.* "I desire to acknowledge, after many days, the volumes 'Kenilworth' and 'Harold,' in the Standard Literature Series. I am much pleased with these books. It is a great service which you are rendering the schools. Our children must read all the British-American classics which have any bearing upon history, and, with all that is absolutely required of them in this day, they *cannot* do what they must do. There is a conflict of 'oughts.' You make it possible, here, for the child to get all he needs of each of all the books he must read. It is a great service. I admire the appreciation of the editors of their text."

C. B. Gilbert, *Superintendent of Schools, Newark, N. J.* "The Standard Literature Series bids fair to prove a most valuable addition to literature available for use in schools. The books are well selected, carefully edited, and supplied with valuable notes and maps. 'Harold, the Last of the Saxon Kings,' may serve as a type. For classes in English history it will prove invaluable, giving, as it does in the language of a master, a most vivid picture of early England; its struggles and its people. The Introduction paves the way for what is to follow. The portions omitted can be spared, and the notes are just enough to clear up difficult passages, but not enough to be burdensome."

R. E. Denfeld, *Superintendent of Schools, Duluth, Minn.* "I have carefully read many of the numbers of the Standard Literature Series and do not hesitate to say that they are exceptionally well edited. One in particular I have in mind which was so carefully condensed as to make it of convenient size for a school reading book, and yet no part of the essentially connected matter was omitted."

Henry R. Sanford, *Institute Conductor for New York State, Penn Yan, N. Y.* "You are doing a good thing in thus giving to the public cheap editions of standard literature."

Correspondence is invited. Special discounts to schools and dealers. Address

University ◆ Publishing ◆ Company

NEW YORK: 43-45-47 East Tenth St.
BOSTON: 352 Washington St.   NEW ORLEANS: 714-716 Canal St.

www.ingramcontent.com/pod-product-compliance
Lightning Source LLC
Chambersburg PA
CBHW021917180426
43199CB00032B/420